The Seventh Way

The Seventh Way

Readings from
THE ALETHEON
The Practice and The Realization
of The Divine Acausal Reality-Principle

BY THE AVATARIC GREAT SAGE,
Adi Da Samraj

THE DAWN HORSE PRESS
MIDDLETOWN, CALIFORNIA

NOTE TO THE READER

All who study the Way of Adidam or take up its practice should remember that they are responding to a Call to become responsible for themselves. They should understand that they, not Avatar Adi Da Samraj or others, are responsible for any decision they make or action they take in the course of their lives of study or practice. The devotional, Spiritual, functional, practical, relational, and cultural practices and disciplines referred to in this book are appropriate and natural practices that are voluntarily and progressively adopted by members of the practicing congregations of Adidam (as appropriate to the personal circumstance of each individual). Although anyone may find these practices useful and beneficial, they are not presented as advice or recommendations to the general reader or to anyone who is not a member of one of the practicing congregations of Adidam. And nothing in this book is intended as a diagnosis, prescription, or recommended treatment or cure for any specific "problem", whether medical, emotional, psychological, social, or Spiritual. One should apply a particular program of treatment, prevention, cure, or general health only in consultation with a licensed physician or other qualified professional.

The Seventh Way is formally authorized for publication by the Free Sannyasin Order of Adidam. (The Free Sannyasin Order of Adidam is the senior Cultural Authority within the formal gathering of formally acknowledged devotees of the Avataric Great Sage, Adi Da Samraj.)

Produced by the Dawn Horse Press,
a division of the Avataric Pan-Communion of Adidam.

International Standard Book Number: 978-1-57097-242-3

CONTENTS

INTRODUCTION

This volume includes readings from one of Avatar Adi Da's primary Revelation-Texts, *The Aletheon: The Practice and The Realization of The Divine Acausal Reality-Principle.* "Aletheon" is a word derived by Adi Da Samraj from the Greek "aletheia", meaning "Truth". Pronounced "ah-LAY-thee-yon" (and, thus, evoking sacred spaces such as the "Pantheon" or the "Parthenon"), the name of this text means "That Which Is (or Contains) the Truth". By referencing the ancient Greek concept of "aletheia", Avatar Adi Da is emphasizing an understanding of a Transcendent "Truth" that is Self-Evident and Self-Revealed, rather than a merely relative or consistent "fact". Indeed, Reality Itself—That Which simply Is—Is Transcendental Spiritual Truth, as Avatar Adi Da Reveals in these pages.

The readings in *The Seventh Way* are among Avatar Adi Da's most sublime and profound Utterances. Everything in this book was originally Spoken by Avatar Adi Da, as spontaneous and ecstatic discourse to His devotees—during the final decade (from mid-1995 to mid-2005) of His immense outpouring of Teaching-Instruction. During Avatar Adi Da's Years of Teaching (from 1972 to 2005), He engaged those who approached Him in thousands of hours of such Instructive Discourse. That great period of Instruction spontaneously came to a point of definitive Fullness in 2005, since which time Avatar Adi Da has ceased to engage the mode of Instructing His devotees by Speaking to them in response to their questions.

Avatar Adi Da's Communication of the seventh stage of life is His Unique Gift to humankind. When He Speaks of the seventh stage of life, He is Speaking of Himself, and Confessing His Own State. Thus, His seventh stage Word allows us to Directly Intuit the Reality That is most perfectly Beyond the ego—the Reality That He I̲s̲. Truly, the Instruction in this volume epitomizes the nature of Avatar Adi Da's Communication in *The Aletheon* as a whole—His unmediated Revelation of Reality and Truth that is the "Seventh Way" He offers to humankind. ■

PART ONE

The Discourse
of
The Seventh Way

The Way of
Zero Bargaining

1.

The only-by-Me Revealed and Given Way of Adidam is not about idealizing any of the first six stages of life. Rather, the only-by-Me Revealed and Given Way of Adidam is a practice and a culture of life that is founded in My Revelation of the seventh stage of life, and not in any lesser stage. Therefore, the only-by-Me Revealed and Given Way of Adidam is the Unique seventh stage Teaching.

The Way of Adidam is not a developmental process of progressing through the stages of life. Rather, the Way of Adidam, from Its beginning, exists in the context of the culture of the seventh stage of life.

The seventh stage of life is My Divine Avataric Self-Nature and Self-Revelation. My seventh stage Revelation and Gift is What the Way of Adidam is about. My seventh stage Revelation and Gift is What the unique practice of the Way of Adidam is for.

I have Described the characteristics of each of the first six stages of life—and I have Described the gross, subtle, and causal dimensions of "experience" (or the total psycho-physical anatomy of the human being) with reference to the first six (or developmental) stages of life. Nevertheless, the Way of Adidam is not, in any sense, about developing the first six stages of life. In fact, the Way of Adidam requires, as a foundation for Its "Perfect Practice", the transcending of the characteristic errors and limitations of each of the first six stages of life.

THE SEVENTH WAY

Therefore, the Way of Adidam does not have the same basis as any of the historical traditions of humankind. All of the historical traditions of humankind are founded in one or more of the developmental (or first six) stages of life. Every one of the historical traditions of humankind is based either on the revelation of a teacher (or teachers) who demonstrated (and gave instructions related to) one or more of the developmental (or first six) stages of life or (otherwise) on collective lore that represents one or more of the developmental (or first six) stages of life. Therefore, all historically-given teachings are to be rightly understood in terms of the actual psycho-physical structures of the human being, as those structures correlate with one or more of the first six stages of life. The fact that each stage of life is uniquely associated with particular psycho-physical structures in the human mechanism is the reason why I Describe Spiritual Masters as being of different degrees and different modes of Realization. The manner of teaching (and of Realization) demonstrated by any particular Realizer of the fourth or the fifth or the sixth stage of life is (necessarily) determined by his or her stage of life.

The Divine Avataric Self-Revelation of My Person, Given by Me to all, Is a Unique Revelation. The Divine Avataric Self-Revelation of My Person Is the Consummation, the Fulfillment, and the Completion of the entire Great Tradition of humankind.

It is possible to understand the totality of human history in terms of the esoteric anatomy of the human being—and it is also possible, using these means, to understand why the Way of Adidam is Unique, why My Revelation is Avataric and of universal significance in the history of the Great Tradition of humankind. Indeed, an important aspect of My Wisdom-Teaching is My Unique Revelation (presented in detail in *The Basket of Tolerance*) of exactly why and how the totality of human cultural history can (and should) be understood to be a single (coherent, but multi-faceted) Great Tradition.

14

Thus, the entirety of human history is a demonstration of the inherent psycho-physical anatomy of the human entity, "situated" within the cosmic domain. Consequently, the Great Tradition of humankind is an unfolding of possibilities that are inherently "mapped" by the human structure.

My Divine Avataric Self-Manifestation here Is Unique.

The Way of Adidam—Which I Alone Reveal and Give— Is Unique.

My Divine Avataric Means Are Unique.

My Divine Avataric Revelation-Teaching Is Unique.

Therefore, to embrace the Way of Adidam in My Divine Avataric Company Is a Unique Opportunity.

The only-by-Me Revealed and Given Way of Adidam Is the Avatarically Self-Revealed Divine Reality-Way, Wherein the ego—which is at the root of the historical Great Tradition in all of its forms—is (Ultimately, Most Perfectly) transcended.

Therefore, the only-by-Me Revealed and Given Way of Adidam Transcends the perspective (or "point of view") in which the Great Tradition of humankind is embedded.

The only-by-Me Revealed and Given Way of Adidam Is the Unique, Perfect, and Ultimate Reality-Way.

The only-by-Me Revealed and Given Way of Adidam is about the by-My-Divine-Avataric-Transcendental-Spiritual-Grace-Given Direct Realization of the Self-Nature, Self-Condition, and Self-State That Is Reality Itself.

2.

The only-by-Me Revealed and Given Way of Adidam is the seventh stage Way, from the beginning—because It is established Prior to egoity, from the beginning.

The Way of Adidam is thus established because It is based on "radical" devotion to Me, founded on the tacit heart-recognition that I Am the Divine Self-Nature, Self-Condition, Source-Condition, and Self-State of all-and-All.

The Position of Reality Itself Is the Position of and <u>As</u> That Which Is Always Already The Case.

Reality Itself <u>Is</u> <u>So</u> now.

Most Ultimately, Reality Itself will be Realized to Be So, and to have Always Already Been So.

Reality Itself Is the Context of <u>all</u> "experiencing".

Reality Itself Is Truth.

Reality Itself Is What is to be Realized—not merely eventually, but always immediately, directly, and tacitly.

That Reality Itself <u>Is</u> Truth Is the Realization Sitting before you, in My Own Person.

The Divine Reality-Way of Adidam is <u>Self</u>-Revealed, in Person, before your eyes.

I <u>Am</u> That Which is to Be Realized.

You must Realize <u>Me</u>.

The Reality-Condition, Self-Revealed to you, must be entered into profoundly—Such That "It" is Realized now and <u>As</u> "It" <u>Is</u>.

The Reality-Condition could be Realized simply by Sighting Me here, in My Avatarically-Born bodily (human) Divine Form.

My "Bright" Divine Self-Nature, Self-Condition, and Self-State could be immediately Obvious to you.

The reason that My "Bright" Divine Self-Nature, Self-Condition, and Self-State is <u>not</u> Obvious to you is that you are bound up in your own errors, your own habits, your own "self"-reflection, your own identification with the body-mind.

The "Bright" Divine State of Reality Itself Is always First, always the Basis of all "experience".

That State is not the condition of bondage in which you characteristically presume to exist.

Reality Itself Is Perfectly Obvious (or Always Already Self-Evident).

Reality Itself is not subject to doubt.

Yet, you dismiss Reality Itself—moment to moment.

Only Reality Itself Is Always Already The Case.

What "It" Is must be Realized—by entering into "It" profoundly.

Reality Itself Is the Root-Condition, or Source-Condition, of all-and-All.

3.

Most Perfect Realization of Reality Itself utterly destroys your egoic life—so watch out! The "trouble" with seventh stage Divine Self-Realization is that there is no "one" left over to enjoy "It"! Therefore, to seek That Realization makes no sense from any conventional "point of view"—because the one who is seeking is the "price" that must be paid in order to Realize "It". You imagine that "you" will enjoy the satisfaction of having achieved Realization, or of having Realization Given to you—but all of that is nonsense. Realization is not something "you" will achieve or enjoy— because the ego is the "price".

Right and true practice of the only-by-Me Revealed and Given Way of Adidam deals with egoity itself, as the fundamental matter to be transcended. However, in the Great Tradition of humankind, even though certain modes of egoity are (as a general rule) addressed, the utter transcending of egoity is not required (or even, altogether, understood). The various schools of the Great Tradition are, characteristically, developmental in nature, exercising the potential of human individuals to achieve certain modes of "experience" (and of presumed Realization), based on the potentials of the structured body-mind. To (thus) strategically exercise any of the potentials of the human psycho-physical structure is (necessarily) to engage an ego-based process. In the esoteric schools of the Great Tradition of humankind, the ego is identified as such, and is (in one manner or another) required to be disciplined and purified—but the ego is not itself most directly transcended. Therefore, in the Great Tradition of humankind, the mechanisms of the mere development of psycho-physical potential are never most perfectly transcended.

Therefore, all of the schools within the historical Great Tradition of humankind are conditional in nature—dependent upon conditional exercises (in one form or another), and dependent on the characteristics of one or more of the first six stages of life.

As a general rule, all authentic traditions and cultures include forms of "self"-discipline relating to the first three stages of life—relating, in other words, to "money, food, and sex" and the social ego. The gross (functional, practical, and relational) characteristics of human existence are, generally speaking, subject to discipline in virtually all authentic traditions and cultures. However, such discipline does not amount to the direct transcending of egoity itself, or the direct transcending of the mechanism of the body-mind itself. In the various schools of the Great Tradition of humankind, the mechanism of the body-mind, and the egoic qualities of the individual, are purified and transformed—but they are never entirely transcended.

The only-by-Me Revealed and Given Way of Adidam is about the (ultimately) most perfect transcending of egoity. Right-life practice in the Way of Adidam demonstrates characteristic signs of purification and transformation—signs (and, also, "experiences") that reflect the various structures of the psycho-physical anatomy—but the Way of Adidam Itself is about the direct transcending of egoity and the (Ultimately, Most Perfect) Realization of the Divine Self-Nature, Self-Condition, and Self-State of Reality Itself (Which Is the "Bright" Itself, My Very Person).

To the degree that the forms of "self"-discipline given in the Great Tradition of humankind are (in a developmental sense) truly purifying and transformative, there is some freeing of energy and attention. Such discipline does release certain modes of energy and attention from certain kinds of egoic patterning. Nevertheless, such discipline is not a matter of the full and direct transcending of egoity itself. In the Great Tradition of humankind, egoity itself is not most fundamentally understood. Therefore, in the Great Tradition of humankind, egoity is not most fundamentally addressed. Traditional forms of "self"-discipline are (as a general rule) developmental, playing upon the structure of the body-mind—whereas the forms of "self"-discipline Given by Me transcend egoity directly and most fundamentally. Right and true practice of the Way of Adidam inherently transcends all of the mechanisms of the conditionally arising body-mind, by tacitly and intrinsically Realizing What Is Self-Evident and Always Already Beyond all conditional arising. Both the foundation and the Perfect seventh stage Realization of the only-by-Me Revealed and Given Way of Adidam are inherently free of dependency upon any and all of the conditional characteristics of the body-mind and anything being done to those characteristics.

The only-by-Me Revealed and Given seventh stage Realization is not a developmental stage of life. The first six stages of life are all, in and of themselves, developmental. In other words, each of the first six stages of life is based on exploiting certain potentials inherent in the structures of the body-mind. The only-by-Me Revealed and Given seventh stage of life is about the utter transcending of the conditional structures of the body-mind. The only-by-Me Revealed and Given seventh stage of life is about the inherent transcending of the entire psycho-physical structure—gross, subtle, and causal. In the context of the only-by-Me Revealed and Given seventh stage of life, there is no dependency whatsoever on that structure.

From the beginning, practice of the only-by-Me Revealed and Given Way of Adidam is the real, "self"-disciplined practice of "radical" devotion to Me. Because the practice of the Way of Adidam is "radical" devotion to Me, that practice is inherently established Beyond (or Prior to) egoity itself, and Beyond (or Prior to) the disposition of seeking to develop any of the psycho-physical potentials of the body-mind. The disposition of right and true practice of the Way of Adidam is always the disposition of Prior "self"-surrender, or the disposition that is Beyond (or Prior to) egoity and Beyond (or Prior to) conditional possibilities.

4.

If you are My devotee, you must be always turned whole bodily to Me. You must always heart-recognize and heart-respond to Me. In due course, you must Transcendentally Spiritually "Locate" Me and "Know" Me. Altogether, you must be profoundly affected by My Divine Avataric Company. You must allow your illusions to be undone. When all of this is (truly effectively) Accomplished by Me, then practice of the only-by-Me Revealed and Given Way of Adidam has become Perfect.

Right now, you appear to be thinking—but that thinking is not actually being done by you (as you Really Are). You are not the thinking mind. Rather, you are simply the formless and actionless mere Witness of whatever is arising. The Witness-Consciousness does not—and, indeed, cannot—think. That Which Is the mere Witness cannot make a thought.

Throughout the many years of My Divine Avataric Teaching-Work and Revelation-Work, I explicitly Told My devotees (and, also, explicitly Showed My devotees, by all My Divine Avataric Means) that none of the purposes of the first six stages of life are the Realization of the Inherently egoless Reality That Is Always Already The Case. Therefore, none of the phenomena of the first six stages of life are Most Ultimate Realization of That Which Is Always Already The Case. There is no form of seeking that leads to Most Perfect

Realization of the Divine Self-Nature, Self-Condition, and Self-State of Reality Itself—none. All seeking is a dramatization of egoity—built upon the illusions of egoity, and serving the purposes of egoity.

Practice in the only-by-Me Revealed and Given Way of Adidam is not a matter of beginning in the context of the first three stages of life, and (then) working (progressively, stage by stage) toward the sixth stage of life, and (then) "doing" the sixth stage of life, only then to (finally) move on to the seventh stage of life. That is exactly what the Way of Adidam is not. The Way of Adidam is not the "great path of return". Rather, the Way of Adidam is, from the beginning, the Way of right and true devotional relationship to Me— living (whole bodily) turned to Me in My Avatarically-Born bodily (human) Divine Form, moment to moment. In the context of that whole bodily devotional turning to Me, you become more and more profoundly affected by My Divine Avataric Self-Revelation of My Person and State—until (in due course) you are entered into My Divine Avataric Self-Revelation in Transcendental Spiritual and (Most Ultimately) Divine terms. My Divine Avataric Self-Revelation is Given to you, by Me. The Realization of Reality Itself is Given to you, by Me. The Way in Which these Gifts are Given to you is the Way of the Divine Heart-Master's Grace.

My Divine Avataric Grace of Person—and, therefore, the practice of turning whole bodily to Me—is not about progressively developing the potentials of any of the first six stages of life, which potentials are the basis of anything and everything in the Great Tradition of humankind. That is what My Revelation is not. My devotees often describe "experiences" of what they presume to be My Influence, but such "experiences" are not Realization. The best they can be is some mode of psycho-physical sensitivity to Me. Even so, it is not the "experiences" that are the point. My Divine Avataric Person is the point.

If you understand My Divine Avataric Teaching-Revelation, you understand that the Way of Adidam is the seventh stage Way, and that It is Such from the beginning—by virtue of total psycho-physical turning to Me. All there is to do relative to the preoccupations of the first three stages of life is to simply turn to Me in all the functional, practical, and relational modes of "money, food, and sex" and social egoity— living by My Instruction in every moment, simply that. The practice of the Way of Adidam is not about being a "case" that you have to "figure out", or a pattern that you must fulfill or perfect. It is simply about turning the four principal faculties to Me and conforming the functional body-mind to Me. Thus, the Way of Adidam is a matter of devotional turning to Me and obedience to My Word and Person.

If that heart-responsive turning to Me and that obedience (or conformity) to My Person (by means of the fulfilling of My Instructions, as I have Given them) become your real and consistent practice, then the foundation practice of Adidam is established readily, in a finite period of time. Virtually anyone can do this. Beyond the student-beginner level, the (necessarily, formal renunciate) practice of the Way of Adidam is about being combined with Me by virtue of My Transcendental Spiritual Self-Transmission of My Own Nature, Condition, and State. By Means of That Transmission, I Conform My devotee to the Self-Nature, Self-Condition, and Self-State of Reality Itself. That Transcendental Spiritual process is Given by Grace of My Divine Avataric Person, in the midst of simple (whole bodily) turning to Me and conformity of life to Me—until My devotee becomes self-evidently established in the "Perfect Practice" of devotion to Me.

Such is the seventh stage Way. Such is the only-by-Me Revealed and Given Way of Adidam. The Way of Adidam is not about spending your lifetime struggling with (or, otherwise, indulging in) the gross characteristics of the body-mind in the context of the first three stages of life. Neither is the Way of Adidam about exoteric dabbling in superficial "religiosity". The Way of Adidam is about real devotional turning to Me, with all the principal faculties—rather than allowing the faculties to be turned to themselves and their patterned contents. This moment to moment practice of the Way of Adidam is purifying, enabling My devotee to become more and more conformed to Me, and to My Spiritual Intrusion (Which directly Awakens My devotee to My State). Heart-Communion with Me, the Divine Avataric Revealer of the seventh stage of life, is what makes the Way of Adidam the seventh stage Way.

5.

Practice of the only-by-Me Revealed and Given Way of Adidam is founded on the devotional recognition-response to Me, or the turning of the four principal faculties to Me. By Its very nature, then, the Way of Adidam is the seventh stage Way—because of My Own Nature and your tacit heart-response to Me. Nevertheless, Adidam is the seventh stage Way in exact coordination (or coincidence) with your degree of maturity in the practice of devotional recognition-response to Me in the any present moment.

If you study My Divine Avataric Word relative to the seventh stage Demonstration of the "Perfect Practice", such study will not (in and of itself) enable you to <u>Realize</u> the seventh stage of life in the any present moment. You can be sympathetic with what I Say about the seventh stage of life, and it can make sense to you, and something may be tacitly convincing about what I Say, but you will not, merely by studying My Divine Avataric Word, be able to <u>Realize</u> the seventh stage of life in the any present moment.

Right and true practice of the Way of Adidam is practice of the seventh stage Way. Nevertheless, you cannot practice the Way of Adidam beyond your capability for demonstration in the any present-time. You cannot practice the Way of Adidam merely on the basis of a philosophical sympathy with My Ultimate Descriptions. You can <u>think</u> that My Descriptions are somehow about you (in present time), but that is just thinking. You cannot <u>practice</u> the Way of Adidam in the context of the seventh stage of life merely on the basis of reading My Divine Avataric Word of Instruction. You cannot <u>Realize</u> the Divine Self-Nature, Self-Condition, and Self-State of Reality Itself merely on the basis of study.

What are you actually up to? What are you actually doing? What is the nature and profundity of your devotional recognition-response to Me? What is your demonstration of that recognition-response? All of <u>that</u> determines the nature and mode of your actual participation in the process of the Way of Adidam.

From the very beginning, practice of the only-by-Me Revealed and Given Way of Adidam, authentically demonstrated, is a demonstration of the seventh stage <u>Way</u>—but the practice of the Way of Adidam that precedes the seventh stage of life is not a demonstration of seventh stage <u>Realization</u>. Seventh stage Realization Perfectly Transcends all brain-states and everything about the body-mind.

6.

The seventh stage Realization, Which is established through the only-by-Me Revealed and Given "Perfect Practice" of the Way of Adidam, is not developed on the basis of any of the first six stages of life. Thus, the seventh stage Realization transcends all psycho-physical dependence, and, thus, all dependence on conditionality.

What is Realized in the seventh stage of life is that the Divine Self-Nature, Self-Condition, and Self-State is, indeed, the Nature, Condition, and State of all phenomena—but not the "cause" of phenomena themselves.

In the orientation of the sixth stage of life, there is a tendency toward solipsism. The disposition of solipsism seems to suggest that the "interior" of the human being is somehow "causing" the universe. A philosopher in the Western tradition, George Berkeley, posed the question, "If a tree falls down in the forest, and no one is there to observe it, does it make any sound?" In other words, is the "subjective" conscious awareness of the individual actually "causing" the universe? If that "subjective" conscious awareness were not there, would there be no universe?

Clearly, without the "subjective" conscious awareness of the individual, there would be no "experience" of the universe—but is the "subjective" conscious awareness the "cause" of the universe? Is the mind actually "causing" the "world"? Or is the mind merely the non-"causative" medium (or mechanism) in which awareness of the "world" arises?

If you enter into the depth of your own personal existence, what do you find at the root? You find Consciousness Itself.

If you examine the structure of any apparent "object"—anything at all—you will get into molecular levels, and atomic levels, and the subatomic levels of quantum physics. Ultimately, everything you can examine about any "object" could be called "light"—although light, by common definition, has a kind of conditionality. It could also be called Energy, or Force—even Non-conditional Force. Therefore, it Is Intrinsically Self-Evident that the "Substantial" Reality-Condition of any apparent "object" is Non-conditional Force (or Energy)—and the "Essential" Reality-Condition of any apparent "subject" (or separate "self"-identity) is Non-conditional Consciousness. Non-conditional Energy and Non-conditional Consciousness may, as descriptions, seem like two different "things", but they are not.

There is only One "Substantial" and "Essential" Reality— Which Is of an Acausal Nature, and of Which everything is a transparent (or merely apparent), and non-necessary, and inherently non-binding modification. Such is the only-by-Me Revealed and Given seventh stage Realization.

The seventh stage Realization Is the Divine Self-Realization of the Self-Nature, Self-Condition, and Self-State of Reality Itself.

The seventh stage Realization Is the Divine Self-Realization of the Intrinsic and Self-Evident egolessness, Non-separateness, Indivisibility, and Non-conditional Nature, Condition, and State of Reality Itself.

The seventh stage Realization Is the Divine Self-Realization of the Conscious Light That Intrinsically Self-Recognizes (and, moment to moment, specifically transcends) any and all apparent "objects".

The seventh stage Realization specifically (and moment to moment) Self-Recognizes any and all apparent "objects" to Be Not-"different", Not-an-"object", and As Self (rather than as not-"self").

The seventh stage Realization Divinely and Perfectly Self-Recognizes and Self-Transcends both egoic "self" (or psycho-physical and separate "subjectivity", or "self"-identity) and apparent "object" (or conditional "world")—In and As egoless Self, Consciousness Itself, Indivisible Conscious Light Itself, Reality Itself, and Self-Evident Real God.

The One ("Substantial", "Essential", Prior, and Non-conditional) Condition of conditions Is the "Bright" Conscious Light Itself, the Divine Self-Nature, Self-Condition, and Self-State of all-and-All.

The language of the sixth stage traditions—with its (characteristically, Advaitic) references to "the Self", and its (characteristically, Buddhist) references to "the essence of mind", and so forth—suggests a "subjective" principle that is "causative" (or, in some traditions, merely and exclusively detached) relative to what is apparently "objective". This is why the error of exclusion (or, in some cases, of antinomian, or "self"-indulgent, behavioral abstractedness) is characteristic

26

of the sixth stage traditions—even those (primarily, Advaitic and Buddhist) traditions that assert independence from psycho-physical efforts and supports.

The only-by-Me Revealed and Given seventh stage Realization is not founded on an exclusionary identification with what is "subjective" to the human being. The seventh stage Realization is the Realization of the Divine Self-Nature, Self-Condition, and Self-State of all-and-All—everything apparently "subjective", and everything apparently "objective". The "subjective" is not the "cause" of the "objective". The "subjective" and the "objective" are, equally, apparent modifications of the same Indivisible Divine Reality.

The "radical" (or "at-the-root") "equivalence" of the "subjective" and the "objective" is a fundamental aspect of the Uniqueness of My seventh stage Revelation. Therefore, the means whereby the only-by-Me Revealed and Given seventh stage Realization is established is not any sixth stage "method" of exclusion, but the direct Revelation of My Own Divine Self-Nature, Self-Condition, and Self-State, by Means of My Transcendental Spiritual Self-Transmission.

In the Way of Adidam, Most Perfect Divine Self-Realization is Established Directly, by Means of My Transcendental Spiritual Self-Revelation—not philosophically, by the exercise of the conditional structures of the body-mind. Therefore, right and true practice of the Way of Adidam does not lead to error-based Realizations, or Realizations that are not yet Perfect (and not altogether Prior to conditionality), or Realizations that are dependent on conditions. Right and true practice of the Way of Adidam does not lead to philosophical errors, or Reality-errors, of any kind.

The "world" is not "caused" by your "inner person", or your mind. Your structures of mind are the apparent means whereby you are perceiving the "world"—from the perspective (or "point of view") of a body-mind. However, your structures of mind are not "causing" the "world". Nor is That

Which Is Always Already The Case "Causing" the "world". The "world" has no "outside cause".

To describe Reality Itself as the "Creative Source" of the "world" requires, first of all, that one presume the error of identifying with what appears to be separate from Reality Itself, or with what is merely conditional. You presume that you are the body-mind, and that the universe (as an "objec-tified" solid something-or-other) exists already—and, then, on that basis, you try to figure everything out. Any notion of a "Creative Source" winds up justifying phenomena, and the "point of view" of conditionality itself. Realization of Reality Itself (Which Is Always Already The Case) begins only from the Position of Reality Itself. Realization of Reality Itself is not something arrived at, or "caused" by, some conditional effort or mode of seeking. Realization of Reality Itself does not depend on any of that. In fact, the only-by-Me Revealed and Given seventh stage Realization of Reality Itself specifi-cally transcends all seeking and all psycho-physical struc-tures (whether gross, subtle, or causal).

When the seventh stage Realization is Awakened, every-thing that arises is Divinely Self-Recognized.

Consciousness Itself does not "create" phenomena.

Indeed, Consciousness Itself has nothing to do with phenomena.

Consciousness Itself Is Always Already Free of phenom-ena, Always Already not limited by phenomena.

Phenomena are not necessary to Consciousness Itself.

Phenomena are only apparently arising as modifications of Consciousness Itself.

Phenomena do not exist because you, as an individual "self", are somehow thinking them into existence.

The phenomenal "world" is not personally "caused", and it is not "caused" by your "God"-idea of a "Creator-Deity" that is merely a gigantic version of yourself.

The universe is not "caused".

There is no "cause".

The universe is apparent only.

The "world" seems to be—but on what basis does it exist? You can begin from your position of noticing what seems, and try to figure it all out. In that case, you eventually wind up justifying the appearance of conditions, and remaining bound to apparent conditions.

Only the Intrinsic Prior Realization of the Divine Self-Nature, Self-Condition, and Self-State of Reality Itself—only the Intrinsic Prior Realization of That Which Is Always Already The Case (and not merely your own "inward self-condition")—Is the Realization of Reality Itself, or Truth Itself, or Real (Acausal) God.

Reality Itself Is Acausal, or Non-causal. In other words, there is no necessity to the universe. If the universe were "caused", there would be some kind of necessity to it—but the universe is not "caused". The universe is apparent only.

Therefore, in the Realization of That Which Is Always Already The Case, there is no otherwise-existing universe or body-mind.

7.

The "world" is not as you perceive the "world" to be, nor as you think the "world" to be, nor as you describe the "world" to be. You do not perceive the "world" As it Is. You perceive the "world" from the "point of view" of your own "location" in time and space. Therefore, you have not even a clue about the Reality-Nature of the "world". You do not need to have the entire universe in front of your eyes at the moment in order to acknowledge your fundamental ignorance.

You do not even see the room you are in As it Is. You can vouch for something about what the apparent room looks like from where you are sitting right now, from the perspective of your eyes, and mind, and perception altogether. You have a perceived "location". You see the room in that mode. You could describe the room at great length—but you would still not be seeing the room As it Is. What does the room actually look like? You never see the totality of the room.

If each person's "point of view" were replaced by a camera, and you collected photographs of all those "points of view" in the room—up, down, sides, all different orientations—and if you put them all together, you would wonder what you were looking at. Ten such photographs would be enough to make the room unrecognizable. In any case, no single photograph represents the room in its totality. Any single photograph is a portrayal (or an abstract representation) only—and the same is true of your perception. Your perception is only a portrayal (or an abstract representation) of the room. Your perception is not the room As it Is.

For this reason, the universe as described by science (or by any other conditional, or psycho-physical, means) is only a portrayal (or an abstract representation) of the universe, according to the currently accepted norms of description. Regardless of how disciplined or how accurate that portrayal is, it is still not true. It cannot be true—because all conditional "knowledge" is limited by the perspective of "point of view". "Knowledge" from any single "point of view" is already reductive—and, therefore, already false. Until you can view the universe from every possible "point of view" in space and time, you are neither perceiving the universe As it Is nor "knowing" the universe As it Is.

What, in fact, does the universe look like from every possible "point of view" in (and beyond) space and time? "Real God" is as good a term as any to describe this "look". To recognize the universe in its Indivisibility, and (otherwise) in its Totality—beyond description, beyond time, and beyond place—is to "Know" the universe in the Divine sense. There is no doubt about the existence of the universe, regardless of how much you "know" or do not "know" about it.

Since you do not "know" the room—or the universe—As it Is, your perceptions are not true to Reality Itself. Your perceptions are merely local, "experiential", and ego-supported (or ego-based). All of the paths in the Great Tradition are, likewise, founded on "point of view". That is what each of the six stages of life is—a "point of view" of the body-mind, conferring its own likeness on the universe. All six of the developmental stages of life are purposed to give power to human "points of view", as means of serving the ego.

Most Perfect (or seventh stage) Divine Self-Realization is the transcending of "point of view" itself—in both directions, whether looking toward the "subjective" (or the "internal") or looking toward the "objective" (or the "external"). Whichever direction one looks, one's looking is based on "point of view".

"Point of view" defines everything about conditional "knowledge", whether it is "knowledge" of "self" or "knowledge" of the universe. That is the purpose served by "point of view". That "knowledge" is the power of "point of view"—its presumed ability to escape bad luck, misfortune, confinement, death, bad results, negative destiny, and so on. That presumed power (or ability) is the purpose of the effort of introversion. It is also the purpose of the effort of extroversion. It is the purpose of all seeking.

The six developmental stages of life are all methods of seeking, based on "point of view". In the human case, "point of view" is identified with the body-mind, and associated with a perceiving and "knowing" of a universe that is felt to have some correspondence to the body-mind. This is true even of science. How could science utter even a word, if there were not some basic presumption that it is possible to "know" about the universe, based on "point of view"?

You cannot see what is behind you. You cannot see the room as it would be seen by somebody in another position in the room. You cannot "know" the room from any position but your own. That being the case, what difference does it make what you "know" about the universe? Whatever you may "know" about the universe, it is nothing but "local knowledge". No matter how far your vision may extend, it is merely the extension of "point of view", with reference to "location" in time and space. No "point of view" is Ultimate. No "point of view" is even in the direction of Ultimate "Knowledge". It is not possible for "point-of-view"-based "knowledge" to achieve Ultimacy.

"Creationist" theories are based on the same flaw. They are expressed from the "point of view" (or perspective) of human individuals, and of the "world" of human beings. According to that "point of view", it is presumed that "God" made what is in front of your eyes, just as it seems. In that kind of naive "religious" view, it is presumed that "God" made the room. But what about the room As it Really Is? Does the room, As it Really Is, have anything to do with you at all? If the room Is As it Is—and it certainly Is—then the room Is As it Is only from all possible "points of view", both in and beyond space and time.

Describing the room As it Is is the same as describing Truth Itself, or Reality Itself. Consciousness Itself—the "Bright", the Divine Conscious Light, the Self-Existing and Self-Radiant Reality—is not merely the "inward" core of the ego-"I". Truth Itself, or Reality Itself, is not "subjective" in the egoic sense. The Truth is not attained or Realized by means of the mechanism of the body-mind. Only in the transcending of the mechanism of body-mind, only in the transcending of all the methods and all the searches built upon the mechanism of the body-mind, only in the transcending of "point of view", is there Ultimacy. Such is the only-by-Me Revealed and Given seventh stage Realization.

The seventh stage of life is not Realized unless and until there is the most perfect transcending of the body-mind, the most perfect transcending of "point of view".

Therefore, notice this: You do not even "know" what the room looks like. That is a very important observation. You do not exhaustively "know" what anything is about. And you certainly do not—and never can—come close to "knowing" What anything Is.

Until Most Perfect (or seventh stage) Divine Self-Realization, there seem to be a lot of rooms, there seems to be "knowledge", and you (yourself) seem to be an "I". Nevertheless, you do not "know" yourself any more than you "know" the room. You do not perceive yourself. You refer to "I", "I", "I" all the time. Every time you speak, you utter the "I"-reference repeatedly. Who are you referring to? Have you ever actually inspected, "located", and defined this person you repeatedly refer to? No, obviously not. There is no such one. You are making a generalized reference to the ego-"I", or the total body-mind. The total body-mind is always happening, always changing, and is not comprehensively definable. Therefore, you never perceive what you call "I", just As it Is. You see something about yourself from the "point of view" of presumed separate identity (or the "point of view" of attention), but you never actually perceive yourself As you Are, from all possible "points of view" in time and space and beyond. Never. You never have. Who Is that?

You do not "know" yourself As you Are. You do not "know" What anything Is. You do not perceive the room As it Is. You are full of absurd presumptions, and you are suffering. You would like a way out of that suffering—and that "way out" is what you call "knowledge". However, merely conditional "knowledge" is not the Truth. No matter how inventive you get—and you can go in any of six stages or directions—none of the six possible stages or directions of ego-effort Realizes the Truth.

There Is One Truth, One Ultimate and Most Perfect Realization. It Is the Realization of That Which Is Always Already The Case. It is not you (or the "I" to which you refer) that will Realize What Is. The Realization of Reality Itself is not a "you"-versus-"object" process or result.

The room (or conditional reality) exists. Real (Acausal) God Exists. Ultimately, they are Realized to Be the Same. Reality Is Real God. Reality Is What the room Is, What anything Is, What anyone Is. Reality Is Who Is. Reality is not "you" in the "inside-of-the-ego" sense. Reality is not merely the platform of separateness, not merely the awareness that looks at the feeling of relatedness. The Reality to be Realized Is Transcendental Spiritual in Nature. The Reality to be Realized is Incomprehensible, Beyond definition. Nevertheless, Reality is Realizable—As My Divine Avataric Gift.

In Reality Itself, the ego has no relevance whatsoever— none. In Reality Itself, the ego has no existence. In Reality Itself, there is nothing but the Divine "Bright" Spherical Self-Domain—Which has not been described, indicated, or Realized in the entire history of the Great Tradition of humankind.

8.

All practice in the Way of Adidam is preparation for the "Perfect Practice" in the context of the only-by-Me Revealed and Given seventh stage of life. Thus, practice in the context of the seventh stage of life is the Perfect beginning of the Way of Adidam—not the end (or the final stage). This sounds like a poetic paradox of some kind, but I am very serious about this. The Way Revealed by Me is the seventh stage Way Itself.

If you were to heart-recognize Me Most Perfectly (without any limitation whatsoever), the seventh stage Way would (thereby) be immediately established. Instead, when I Speak of the seventh stage demonstration, it sounds to you like some futuristic possibility. Thus, you are actually thinking in terms of a "way" that is a form of the search. Such is an ego-made revision of the Way of Adidam, an ego-made revision of the Truth, an ego-made "way" of progression toward Most Perfect Realization—as if the body-mind, after some period of time, some period of effort, some period of practice, some period of devotion and surrender, becomes Most Perfectly Realized. Of course, this does not happen. The body-mind (or the ego) never becomes the Realizer of Reality. The body-mind (or the ego) never Realizes the Divine Self-Nature, Self-Condition, Source-Condition, and Self-State of Reality Itself. The body-mind (or the ego) does not Realize Me.

That Which Is to Be Realized—the One Who Is here, Divinely Avatarically Self-Revealed before your eyes in the form of This Body—Is Always Already The Case.

No seeking for Me is fruitful.

No seeking for Me is necessary.

That Which is to be Realized is not an end-phenomenon.

Most Perfect Divine Self-Realization cannot be "caused".

Most Perfect Divine Self-Realization cannot be achieved.

Most Perfect Divine Self-Realization is, necessarily, a Gift—from Me.

The Divine Self-Nature, Self-Condition, and Self-State of Reality Itself Is Always Already The Case, and is Realized by Means of My Divine Avataric Transcendental Spiritual Grace, as a Divine Gift.

Most Perfect Divine Self-Realization is not associated with any "cause-and-effect" process whatsoever.

I (Myself) Am the Avataric Self-Revelation of Most Perfect Divine Self-Realization.

I Speak to you Directly As Such.

I Am here before you As Such.

In the Most Perfect Self-Realization of Reality Itself, renunciation and Realization are simultaneous. It is because of this equation between renunciation and Realization that "Narcissus" wants to bargain with Me. You (as the ego-"I") like the idea of Most Perfect Realization of Divine Love-Bliss-Happiness. That sounds good to anybody. You want Most Perfect Divine Self-Realization—but you do not want to renounce all forms of attachment to conditional existence, as the "price" for such Realization. For you, renunciation has to have a gradual (or progressive) characteristic. Therefore, Realization has to be at the end of a gradual process—while you, in present time, are focused on identification with the body-mind.

What is renounced in the Way of Adidam? The practice of the Way of Adidam is the renunciation of egoity. You do not mind the idea of egolessness. However, when I Indicate that the ego is not an entity but an activity, that the total body-mind is the whole bodily action of "self"-contraction—in other words, when I Indicate that renunciation in the Way of Adidam is renunciation of identification with the body-mind—your "stop lights" start flashing immediately. No—you do not want that. Your attitude immediately becomes, "Just wait a second here. What price are You Talking about now? You are Talking everything, right? I have to give up everything?" That is one way of putting it—but, in fact, renunciation in the Way of Adidam is not about giving up everything—because, in Truth, there is nothing! It is simply that renunciation and Realization coincide in the "Incident" (you may call it) of Most Perfect Divine Self-Realization of Reality Itself.

In the case of My devotees, renunciation does not need to be "achieved" in some progressive sense, whereby you eventually become an ascetical "self"-renouncer who, by that means, "causes" Realization. That is not true renunciation. The idea that renunciation "causes" Realization is a false notion. Nevertheless, Realization Is perfect renunciation. If you were to heart-recognize Me without limitation, you would not only Realize Me (Most Perfectly, and Inherently), you would also become a renunciate on the spot.

There would be no more bargaining about "money, food, and sex" and social egoity—zero bargaining.

The seventh stage Way (in Its fullest true demonstration) begins with such Most Perfect Realization. In other words, the seventh stage Way (in Its fullest true demonstration) begins with Most Perfect renunciation. The seventh stage Way (in Its fullest true demonstration) is the Way of Prior Self-Abiding Divine Self-Recognition of all conditions (in the instant of their arising). The seventh stage Way is not about presuming to be the body-mind and struggling with that presumption. Instead, the seventh stage Way (in Its fullest true demonstration) Is Divine Self-Abiding, Being (without "difference") As the Divine Self-Nature, Self-Condition, and Self-State of Reality Itself, simply Divinely Self-Recognizing whatever arises as the apparent body-mind and the apparent "world"—such that, effectively, there is no body-mind, and there is no "world". That is the fullest true demonstration of the seventh stage Way—the Way of (Priorly Established) Most Perfect Realization and (Priorly Established) Most Perfect renunciation.

The Disposition of that Demonstration is not one of being the body-mind—and, therefore, being bound by the body-mind, or being troubled by the body-mind, or having questions about the body-mind, or wanting to prolong the patterns, the plans, and the seeking that are based on that presumed identification with the body-mind. The first six stages of life are about all of that. As My devotee, you are involved in a Way that is about intrinsically (and, thus, always Priorly) transcending the six developmental stages of life. As My yet maturing devotee, you are always to be transcending the impediments to the seventh stage of life—not merely struggling in the context of the first six stages of life. That is why the Way of Adidam is the seventh stage Way—a Way inherently different from all the modes of the conventional search, which are traditionally associated with the first six stages of life.

The preparatory practice of the Way of Adidam is about transcending the six developmental stages of life, and (thereby) "wearing out" egoic identification with the body-mind—until the only-by-Me Revealed and Given "Perfect Practice" of the Way of Adidam is (by Means of My Divine Avataric Transcendental Spiritual Grace) Established. Then the "Perfect Practice" of Identification with Consciousness Itself, rather than with the body-mind, must be manifested as a true profundity, until seventh stage Realization—which, necessarily and inherently, coincides with most perfect renunciation. Then the Way of Adidam begins—in Its True Divine Fullness.

The "Bright" Is My Revelation.

The "Bright" Is, Inherently and Always Priorly, My Realization.

Realization of the "Bright" is not progressive.

Realization of the "Bright" Is always Intrinsic, Tacit, and Immediate.

Realization of the "Bright" Is, Inherently, Most Perfect.

Therefore, there is no "method" for Most Perfectly Realizing Reality Itself.

There Is Only My Divine Avataric Transcendental Spiritual Grace—and the (necessarily simultaneous) Most Perfect Realization and Most Perfect renunciation that are the Evidence of your reception of My Divine Avataric Transcendental Spiritual Grace and of My Divine Avataric Self-Revelation.

That Is the Way I have Revealed and Given. All aspects of the preparatory practice of the Way of Adidam are a process—Given in "Consideration" with you, based on your present-time insistence on identification with the body-mind, and your consequent present-time unavailability to My Most Perfect Divine Avataric Self-Revelation of Realization and renunciation by Divine Avataric Transcendental Spiritual Grace.

Most Perfect Realization is (Inherently) Demonstrated as Most Perfect renunciation. On this basis, there is the Unique Process of the only-by-Me Revealed and Given seventh stage of life in the Way of Adidam, Which is the unfolding Demonstration of Inherently Perfect Divine Self-Realization. That Demonstration Is Inherently Perfect renunciation, or Most Perfect Non-identification with the body-mind. The seventh stage Demonstration is based upon Prior Realization of That Which Is Always Already The Case—rather than being based on any procedure that, in due course, becomes Most Perfect and (necessarily) Prior Realization (or Realization of That Which Is Always Already The Case).

Because of your attachment to the body-mind "point of view", you are refusing the implications of the apparent requirement of renunciation. As a result, you continue identifying with the body-mind. This is a refusal of the Priorly Perfect and Always-Already-The-Case Realization of Reality Itself. The Realization of Reality Itself is not the end-phenomenon of the Way of Adidam. Rather, the Realization of Reality Itself is the beginning of the Way of Adidam. Therefore, even the right and true practice of turning the faculties to Me is (effectively) That Realization, tacitly confessed—even though the body-mind identification lags behind, and requires this preparatory practice (which I have Elaborated for your sake).

The preparatory practice of the Way of Adidam is not untrue, and it is not the same as the search that is the basis of the six developmental stages of life. The preparatory practice of the Way of Adidam is not (itself) a search, but it is a process that precedes Most Perfect Realization. The preparatory practice of the Way of Adidam is also not inherently necessary—but it is what I must Give to egos because egos insist upon a preparatory practice.

Your Real Status Is That of Consciousness Itself—Which is not "causing" (or even doing) anything whatsoever, Which is not watching (or observing) in any conditional sense, Which has no psycho-physical identity, Which is Inherently Free of all such identity, Which has no involvement in "self"-contraction whatsoever, for Which there is no body-mind, for Which there are no gross, subtle, or causal dimensions of conditional existence, for Which there is no conditional existence whatsoever, no cosmic domain, no "world", no limitation. Consciousness Itself Is Inherently Free and Inherently Perfect.

Consciousness Itself Is Self-Existing and Self-Radiant.

Consciousness Itself is not "within" you.

Consciousness Itself is not "behind" the body-mind, or "deep in" the body-mind.

It is not that you, as My devotee, must progress through the body-mind, in order to discover Consciousness Itself when you get to the end of the potentials of the body-mind. That notion of the Way is an ego-based metaphor for a Way to Reality that is created by the body-mind's perspective (or "point of view").

The body-mind is not the means (or the connection) to Reality Itself (or the Divine Self-Nature, Self-Condition, and Self-State Itself).

Reality Itself Is Self-Existing and Self-Radiant—Always Already The Case.

Most Perfect Divine Self-Realization Is Prior Realization of That Which Is Always Already The Case.

Most Perfect Divine Self-Realization is not the result of a process in which you are being non-Realization and looking toward Realization.

Most Perfect Divine Self-Realization is not a result of working toward Reality.

Most Perfect Divine Self-Realization is not a matter of progressively eliminating anything, or "causing" anything, or proceeding toward a goal.

Most Perfect Divine Self-Realization Is As Is—Just So, Priorly, Perfectly, and Always Already.

Most Perfect Divine Self-Realization Is (Inherently) Most Perfect renunciation, because Realization is Always Already not identified with the body-mind.

There is <u>no</u> equation between Reality Itself and conditional appearances—no equation whatsoever. Reality Itself is <u>not</u> the "Creator" (or "Cause") of conditions. The Status of conditions is Self-Evident when there is Most Perfect Divine Self-Realization of Reality Itself. I <u>Am</u> That Which is to be Realized. My devotee who Most Perfectly Realizes Me is no longer the body-mind, no longer the named ego. When I am Most Perfectly Realized, there is no body-mind, there are no energies, there are no visions, there is no thought. That does not mean that thought is silenced <u>first</u>—in order to Realize Me. Rather, Most Perfect Realization of Me Is Realization of That Which Is Prior to thought. You do not stop thoughts and <u>then</u> enter into Realization of Me. No—you simply (or tacitly, or mindlessly) Realize <u>Me</u>. When Most Perfect Realization of Me is the Case, thoughts are not already there. To Realize Me Most Perfectly is to Abide in the Condition That Is Always Already The Case, the Condition That Is (therefore) Always Already Prior to thought, Prior to body-mind, Prior to everything gross or subtle or causal, Prior to <u>all</u> phenomena—<u>altogether</u> Prior. It is not that thoughts are quieted. It is not that you dissociate from thoughts. Nothing is done to thoughts—because they are not relevant to the Realization of Reality Itself. For My devotee who has Most Perfectly Realized Me, All There <u>Is</u> Is <u>Me</u>. There is no phenomenal characteristic whatsoever in Most Perfect Realization of Me.

It is a Paradox. My devotee who has Most Perfectly Realized Me is walking and talking, and (yet) the seventh stage Process is being Demonstrated. How can that be? There is no satisfactory conventional explanation, any more than there is a satisfactory conventional explanation for how I "Meditate" everyone (even when they are not physically near Me). You can come up with words that may sound plausible, or somehow orderly enough to suggest an accounting for this Process—but no such description is equivalent to the Revelation Itself.

There is a seventh stage Demonstration, as I have Described. That seventh stage Demonstration is the Demonstration of Most Perfect Realization of Me and of Inherently Perfect renunciation and Inherently Perfect Non-identification with the body-mind. That seventh stage Demonstration Is the Way of Adidam.

What is all the Teaching, then, Which I have Given to My devotees relative to the process of the Way of Adidam? It is a Discourse, a "Play", among those who came to Me—asking questions, and living their ordinary lives and presumptions. I Addressed those questions and those presumptions based on Sympathetic Regard. I Entered into the Work of Teaching-through-Submission, the Work of Revelation-through-Compassionate-Regard-of-all—and, by that very process, I have utterly Revealed (to all) the inherent limitations, and the inherent falseness, of all conditional possibilities.

I have Given My devotees a practice founded in the devotional recognition-response to Me, a practice that (in due course) manifests as Prior renunciation and as the Perfect transcending of the various presumptions (or limitations) of the first six stages of life—the stages of life that are built into the mechanism of the body-mind, as it appears conditionally. That practice is not in the likeness of the "great path of return". Rather, that practice is Given (by Me) as a Response to My devotees, as My devotees have come to Me. That by-Me-Given practice is a Compassionate Response to those whose Realization of Me is not yet Most Perfect. My Teaching-Work of Submission was not a Response to the characteristics, and the questions, and all the communications of people who were Realizing Me, but of people who were not Realizing Me. Thus, all I Gave was Given (by Me) as Help for My devotees (in their then present-time disposition) to transcend their limitations—not to feed their mind and their delusion, not to comfort them in their illusions, or to merely console them, or to create a cult of bondage (full of believers' absurdities and ego-possessed presumptuousness) that would merely wind up duplicating the fault inherent in the Great Tradition of humankind. Not that at all. Whatever the Character of My Communication may be in any moment, It is always Intended (Responsively) to Liberate My devotees from the bondage they are manifesting.

What is the purpose of the course of preparatory practice in the Way of Adidam? It is for the sake of establishing the "Perfect Practice" in its primary form—that of the seventh stage Realization as a Way.

I <u>Am</u> the Revelation.

I have Revealed the Truth—and I <u>Am</u> the Revelation of the Truth.

I <u>Am</u> That Truth.

The Truth is Given by Me, Directly.

The Truth is Given by Me without transition, without medium, without "cause".

I am not here to "<u>cause</u>" Realization in you.

I <u>Am</u> the Acausal and Most Perfect Realization of the Truth That <u>Is</u> Reality Itself.

Therefore, you must recognize Me—and, by your devotional response to Me, be utterly given to Me, such that you (Ultimately) Realize Me Most Perfectly.

In Most Perfect Realization of Me, there is not a trace of egoity, not a trace of status, not a trace of body-mind. Realization of Me has no content or status whatsoever. There is nothing to claim in Most Perfect Realization of Me. To Realize My "Bright" Divine Self-Nature, Self-Condition, and Self-State is to be Lost in the Divine, Found in the Divine, Relieved of all seeking, Relieved of all transitions, all means, all purpose.

The seventh stage of life <u>is</u> the Way of Adidam—not any of the first six stages of life. For you who are insisting upon separate "self", I have Given you the preparatory Means whereby the process of the Way of Adidam shows itself

43

Most Perfectly, in due course. However, I have not hidden My Ultimate Teaching. My seventh stage Revelation is Given from the beginning. The Revelation of seventh stage Realization is here in My Very Person. I am Speaking plainly to you now, and I have always Done So.

The seventh stage of life is the Way of Adidam. What you are practicing, what has been Given to you as a Gift in your limitation of presumption, your egoity, will enable you (as a devotee of Mine) to manifest the foundation for Most Perfect Realization and Most Perfect (and motiveless) renunciation.

Most Ultimately, there is simply Divine Self-Abiding.

Does the Condition That Is Divine Self-Abiding do "money, food, and sex"? No.

Does the Condition That Is Divine Self-Abiding meditate? No.

What do you do in order to Realize, then?

You do not do anything—because there is no "you".

Then how, one might ask, do I, in My Divine Self-Realization, continue to Move around, and Talk, and so on? Will My seventh stage devotees move around, and talk, and so on? Probably. Body-minds go on, the "world" goes on, but the State of the seventh stage Realizer is Most Perfect.

My seventh stage devotee can notice what is apparent to others as phenomenal arising—but My seventh stage devotee Divinely Self-Recognizes all conditions as the Divine Self-Nature, Self-Condition, and Self-State of Reality Itself, such that all conditions are simply "Brighter" and "Brighter"— in due course, to the absolute degree of Divine Indifference. Most Ultimately, there is the Outshining of conditional existence itself—in Which there is no "cause" for the continuation of the appearance of conditions.

Renunciation is a spontaneous manifestation of the Intrinsic Samadhi (or Inherently Perfect State) of Most Perfect Divine Self-Realization—the psycho-physical patterning simply loses its motive-center. The manifestation of the seventh stage of life is not such that, after Realization, psycho-physically patterned life merely continues unchanged, until life is just "over" in the natural sense. Rather, in the case of the Realization of the seventh stage of life, the seed of all psycho-physical destiny, egoity itself, is transcended—and the seed of the psycho-physical motion to fulfill conditional purposes is vanished. It all simply falls to the ground and comes unraveled, in Self-Abiding Divine Self-Recognition of all conditions. Such is the characteristic of the seventh stage Demonstration.

Divine Transfiguration, Divine Transformation, and Divine Indifference are the phases of the unraveling of the structure of conditional appearance. It is not that there is a conditional entity doing something. There is no entity. There is no ego. There is simply the body-mind itself (as it appears to others) in the midst of the "world", but there is no "one" behind the body-mind.

The Realization of the seventh stage of life is without conditional characteristic. The Realization of the seventh stage of life is not the "cause", or seed, of any conditional event. That is why the seventh stage Demonstration spontaneously becomes Divine Translation. Divine Translation is the Most Ultimate Unraveled Demonstration. Divine Translation Is the Intrinsic and Perfect Vanishing of the conditional domain. Divine Translation Is the Eternal Stand in My Divine "Bright" Spherical Self-Domain, without "difference". Divine Translation is Trans-"Location" into the "Midnight Sun".

What is That? You will have to find out.

The "Midnight Sun" is not merely the vision of Light at the end of the tunnel at death. What occurs at death are conditional events. The "Midnight Sun" has nothing to do with such conditionality.

The "Midnight Sun" Is the Unique Divine Revelation of My Divine "Bright" Spherical Self-Domain.

The "Midnight Sun" Is Me, the Conscious Light of Reality Itself.

I Am.

I Am Always Already.

There is no one else.

There Is Only One (Indivisible, Self-"Bright", Self-Radiant, Self-Existing, and Always-Already-The-Case) Divine Self-Nature, Self-Condition, and Self-State.

The One and Only Divine Self-Nature, Self-Condition, and Self-State is neither related nor separate.

There is no "difference".

All "difference" is Inherently Divinely Self-Recognizable in Me.

What does that suggest? That there are conditions existing which must first be Recognized, such that they then vanish? No, that is not it. The Divine Self-Nature, Self-Condition, and Self-State Is One and Only. Divine Self-Recognition is a characteristic of Divine Self-Abiding—not a process in the "subject–object" context of separateness, relatedness, otherness, and "difference".

All of your thinking is defeated by these paradoxes. All of your "experiences"—present, past, potential—are not "It".

"Consider" this: Everything you have ever "experienced"—even what you felt was, somehow or other, My Divine Avataric Transcendental Spiritual Self-Transmission—is really not "It", really not Me.

I Am Only.

All "experiencing" is conditional, temporary, and "self"-deluded—all of it.

My Divine Avataric Transcendental Spiritual Self-Transmission cannot be reduced to "experiences" that are incorporated into the body-mind and its egoic disposition.

Be My devotee—that is all.

If you are My devotee, I will Reveal Myself to you Most Perfectly.

Live by My Instruction—and presume nothing.

Treat anything and everything that arises as conditional "experience" as if it were garbage—not contemptuously, but with the understanding that conditional "experience" is never the egoless (and "point-of-view"-less) State That Is Reality Itself.

If you understand Me truly, then you understand that the only-by-Me Revealed and Given Way of Adidam Is the seventh stage Way Itself.

It is not that the Way of Adidam is only suggestively seventh stage at the beginning, becoming Most Perfect only eventually.

The only-by-Me Revealed and Given Way of Adidam is not a process that takes place in the context of the developmental stages of life.

The Way of Adidam Is the seventh stage of life.

The seventh stage of life is the Way I have Revealed and Given, without any preliminary address to the limitations of devotees who are not yet recognizing Me Most Perfectly.

There is still the preparatory culture of Adidam, which exists for the sake of everyone's practice, and all of My Wisdom-Teaching applies to everyone in that culture.

However, you must understand that there is the Constant Offering of the Divinely Self-Realized Process That Is the Way of Adidam.

I am Always Revealing the Way of Adidam Most Perfectly—without beginning, without end.

The seventh stage Reality-Way is What I Reveal to you, What I Call you to embrace.

The seventh stage Reality-Way is what I Make possible by Means of My Compassionate Regard of you.

My Offering is here for all.

Most Perfect Divine
Self-Awakening To
The Domain of Conscious Light

1.

AVATAR ADI DA SAMRAJ: The "Perfect Practice" of the only-by-Me Revealed and Given Way of Adidam (Which is the One and Only by-Me-Revealed and by-Me-Given "Radical" Way of the Heart) is a process of an entirely non-egoic nature. It is a process in Depth. It is always taking place at an in-Depth level. It is always taking place at the level of Consciousness Itself.

There is not anything deeper. There is no deeper than That to go.

The only-by-Me Revealed and Given Process of the "Perfect Practice" takes place in the Domain of Consciousness Itself—moment to moment, always. In the "Perfect Practice" of the Way of Adidam, there is always this in-Depth Process, Prior to the patterning of ego-"I". That Process is most profound in the relative repose of the formal setting of "Perfect Contemplation", but the same Process also continues in the midst of activity.

The only-by-Me Revealed and Given "Perfect Practice" of the Way of Adidam Always Already Stands Prior to and Beyond the limitations of the first six (or developmental) stages of life.

The Way of Adidam is a Process wherein, Most Ultimately, there is Awakening Beyond the first six stages of life, to the seventh stage of life—the most ultimate stage of life, the

Divinely Self-Awakened stage of life—in which there is no egoic limitation whatsoever, no limitation at any level (gross, subtle, or causal), no egoity at all, no pattern of egoity effective at any level whatsoever. The seventh stage Realization is utterly Non-dependent, Inherent in Reality Itself. Therefore, the seventh stage Realization is Most Fundamental.

When I Speak of the seventh stage of life as Beyond the sixth stage of life, and My Own Wisdom-Teaching and Divine Avataric Self-Revelation as Beyond the sixth stage of life, I am Talking not merely about the seventh stage of life Standing Beyond the practices, the philosophies, and the culture traditionally associated with the sixth stage of life. Rather, I am Talking about the seventh stage of life Standing Beyond the limit on Realization that is inherent in the sixth stage of life—whatever particular approach may traditionally be made to the sixth stage of life. The mode of Samadhi (or Realization) possible in the sixth stage of life is approached from different directions in various branches of the Great Tradition—but, inherent in all of those approaches is a particular limit (or error) that is characteristic of the sixth stage of life itself. And that limit is shown most particularly not merely in the philosophy and the practices associated with the sixth stage of life, but in the Realization that is traditionally regarded as the <u>fulfillment</u> of the sixth stage of life. In other words, there is an inherent limitation even in Jnana Nirvikalpa Samadhi, as It may be potentially (but, necessarily, conditionally) Realized in the traditional context of the sixth stage of life.

In the only-by-Me Revealed and Given Way of Adidam, the characteristic Samadhis are of a <u>Non-conditional</u> and <u>Transcendental</u> <u>Spiritual</u> Nature, Unique to My Divine Avataric Self-Revelation and My Avatarically Self-Transmitted Divine Transcendental Spiritual Gift. <u>Priorly</u> <u>Self-Abiding</u> Jnana Nirvikalpa Samadhi—Which <u>Is</u> Prior Self-Abiding in the egoless Root-Context of Amrita Nadi—is the Culmination of the "Perfect Practice" in Its "horizontal" dimension. Non-conditionally Self-Abiding Jnana Nirvikalpa Samadhi is the prerequisite for the subsequent Priorly Ascended Nirvikalpa Samadhi—Which Is Prior Self-Abiding in the egoless and Non-conditionally "Regenerated" Context of Amrita Nadi, and, Thus, egoless Self-Abiding Prior to all, necessarily conditional, modes of Yogic "descent and ascent" in the context of the body-mind. Priorly (and, Thus, Non-conditionally) Ascended Nirvikalpa Samadhi is the Culmination of the "Perfect Practice" in Its "vertical" dimension. The Co-Incidence of both Priorly Self-Abiding Jnana Nirvikalpa Samadhi and Priorly Ascended Nirvikalpa Samadhi—or the Perfect Transcendental Spiritual Self-Establishment of the Totality of Amrita Nadi (in both Its "horizontal" and Its "vertical" dimensions)—is the prerequisite (or the necessary Context) for the only-by-Me Revealed and Given seventh stage Awakening.

The seventh stage Awakening is Prior to and Beyond the final barrier to "Perfect Knowledge" of Reality Itself—the barrier (or the psycho-physically enacted presumption) of "difference". Thus, the seventh stage Awakening is Prior to and Beyond the barrier of the non-Recognizability of the "world" and the illusion (or ego-based presumption) that the "world" is "not-self".

In the traditional process of practice in the course of the first six stages of life, one of the fundamental philosophical principles that is generally instilled in people is that the "world" is "not-self". Traditional practitioners go through a great deal of "self"-discipline in order to get out of the habit of thinking that they are the "world". To get out of the habit of such (literal) "worldliness", they work very hard to achieve a position of (strategic) detachment—a position in which, by feeling detached from the "world", they feel no longer bound to the "world", no longer driven by desires for the "things" of the "world". This position of (strategic, and, therefore, egoic) detachment makes it possible for such traditional

51

practitioners to enter into a sixth stage mode of introversion and Samadhi—a mode that is intended to go beyond all that is (presumed to be) "not-self".

However, no matter how profound the conditional sixth stage Samadhi becomes, it is (nevertheless) a Samadhi that is complicated by the presumption that there is such a thing as "not-self". Thus, in the traditional Samadhi of the sixth stage of life, there is a limit on Realization, a limit on Happiness. Indeed, Happiness Itself may be part of the "not-self" that is left behind, in the traditional sixth stage practitioner's effort to go beyond "not-self"!

This is the reason why some traditional sixth stage dispositions are rather grim—the "point" of attention pressed up against an infinitely dense mass of nothingness. In some traditional sixth stage practices, one is dashed against that nothingness so profoundly that the "point" of attention is fractured uniformly, over the entire surface of a nothingness that covers all.

Such traditional approaches to the practice of the sixth stage of life have, in a few (exceedingly rare) cases, led to the Realization of sixth stage "Sahaja Nirvikalpa Samadhi"— but the Awakening That Characterizes the seventh stage of life Stands entirely Prior to and Beyond even the limitation of sixth stage "Sahaja Nirvikalpa Samadhi".

Your Real Situation is non-egoic. Your Real Situation Is Prior to and Beyond the "point-of-view"-based persona of the waking state, and that of the dreaming state, and that of the sleeping state. Your Real Situation Is the Domain of Consciousness Itself, the Domain of That Which Is Always Already The Case—no matter what arises, and whether or not anything arises. That Self-Condition—the "Self", if you like—is Beginningless and Endless, and Always Already The Case. Surely, That Is Truly "Self" (with a capital "S"). No mere conditional persona, or ego-"I", is True Self. Consciousness Itself Is True Self. Only That Is True Self. Only That Is the

True Self-Position, the True Self-Nature, the True Self-Condition, and the True Self-State of Reality Itself.

In the history of the Great Tradition of humankind, the True Self has characteristically been thought of as "the Self over against something else". Whatever that "something else" may be presumed to be (the "world", or the body, or whatever), it is (necessarily) identified as the "not-Self". This categorization of Reality into "Self" and "not-Self" is the fundamental basis for dualistic thinking (or dualistic presumptions).

The Nature of Consciousness Itself must be found out, must be Realized—because That Is your Real Position. Likewise, the nature of all apparent "objects" must be found out—because you are inevitably associated with apparent "objects".

If you examine any thing that you would describe as "object" to you (following it down to its depth-level, or through a chain of "causation", or however you may like to think about it), eventually it is found to be Light (or Energy)—Whatever That Is. Light (or Energy) Is a Single "Something"—a Force, a kind of Radiation. You cannot reduce an "object" any further than That.

Similarly, if you go within yourself, examining all the layers of your own "you"-description—entering into the in-depth mind, and so on—when you get to the Root of "you", There Is Consciousness, and you cannot go any further than That. You cannot reduce the "subjective you" any further than That. You cannot break Consciousness up into parts. It Is just What It Is. And the same is true of Energy (or Light). No matter how you examine Energy, there is no basis for dividing It.

Thus, all "objects" that you examine turn out to be Energy Itself—and all "subjective" inwardness, entered into, leads you to Consciousness Itself. Therefore, there are two Great Factors discoverable by investigation: Energy Itself and Consciousness Itself. They seem to be different from one another, because you have taken the "point-of-view"-position of the body-mind. On the one hand, you have entered into the "interior" of the body-mind—and, on the other hand, you are constantly moving outward (from the "interior") toward what appears to be "exterior" (or in relation) to the body-mind. And, in your examination of "interior" and "exterior", you have not taken a single route. Or have you?

In any case, when you examined the apparently "subjective interior" and the apparently "objective exterior", you came to the conclusion that one was "self" and the other was "not-self"—and, ultimately, this investigation leads to the conclusion that "interior" (or "self") is Consciousness and "exterior" (or "not-self") is Energy.

But Consciousness is the basis of your examination and "consideration" and judgement of both "interior" and "exterior", both "self" and "not-self". In other words, even that which is identified as "not-self" is something you "know" in the Domain of Consciousness. Thus, the "not-self" is something you "Know"—and, in that sense, the "not-self" is Consciousness. So how can it be "not-self"?

If existence is presumed to be "divided" into "you" and "objects", then that which is "experienced" is presumed to be "not-you", "not-self". Such is the nature of "experience"— as described by (apparently) individual beings. Such is not, in Truth, the Nature of Reality—but beings "experience" their lives as if the Nature of Reality were such. And why is that the case—since Reality is otherwise? Why is it that the common "experience" of beings does not correspond to the actual Nature of Reality?

DEVOTEE: Why do we first presume separation between "self" and "not-self"?

AVATAR ADI DA SAMRAJ: Why are you speaking?

The Single Persisting Factor—whether you are waking, dreaming, or sleeping—Is Consciousness Itself. With respect to anything arising, Consciousness Itself Is in the Position of the Mere Witness. Not the position of attention—but the Position of the Mere Witness. In the three common states (of waking, dreaming, and sleeping), everything is "object" to Consciousness. Everything! You are equipped with faculties of bodily, emotional, mental, and psychic awareness, whereby certain kinds of psycho-physical "objects" are "known"—but even these (apparently "subjective") faculties are "object" to Consciousness. Even attention itself is "object" to Consciousness. Consciousness Stands As the Mere Witness. Therefore, Consciousness is not "the faculties over against the objects".

To Summarize this matter once again: In your usual mode of thinking as the social persona, there is what is "inside" the body-mind, and there is everything "outside" the body-mind. The "inside" is "I", and the "outside" is "not-'I'". But if you examine your actual Position most profoundly, you discover that even the body-mind is something relative to which you are simply the Mere Witness. Therefore, the body-mind is not "you"—just as none of the conditions observed or noticed or perceived by the body-mind are "you".

Thoughts are "object" to you. They arise, and you notice them with attention. Anything that arises to attention is an "object" of attention. You are that which is on the "other side" of attention—somehow "opposite" to "objects" (it seems), because you are on the "other side" of attention, rather than in the sphere of the "objects" of attention. That apparent "opposition" inevitably suggests that Consciousness does not exist in the domain of "objects", that Consciousness exists only on the "interior" side of attention.

From the "point of view" of the sixth stage of life, Consciousness is on the "interior" side of attention. From the "point of view" of the sixth stage of life, Consciousness is a Domain that necessarily excludes the "world" (or the "objects" of attention)—and, therefore, the traditional sixth stage effort is to enter into the Domain of Consciousness in that characteristic "world"-excluding manner, precisely <u>because</u> <u>of</u> the inability to Divinely Self-Recognize the "objects" of attention. In general, you presume that the "objects" of attention are "not-self"—unless the "object" of attention is the body-mind, in which case you say that it is "self". But in neither case is your presumption true.

No matter what arises, you do not "know" What it <u>Is</u>— What it <u>Is</u>! You can say all kinds things about it. You can investigate it on and on and on. You can even <u>say</u> it is Light—but you still do not "<u>know</u>" What it <u>Is</u>. The "knowing" is not the "knowing" of the "<u>Is</u>" part. It is just "knowing" about the "objective", observable whatever.

You do not "know" <u>What</u> any thing <u>Is</u>. So What <u>Is</u> it? You are not in a position to inspect its Existence. You can inspect everything else. Or, to state it differently: You are not in a position to inspect its Consciousness. You are in a position to inspect everything else. You are in a position to inspect signs that <u>suggest</u> there may be Consciousness. But you cannot inspect the Consciousness "objectively"—and, therefore, you cannot "prove" It.

When the habits associated with the binding of attention to the body-mind are gone beyond, then the "Perfect Practice" of the Way of Adidam begins. The "Perfect Practice" is practice in the Domain of Consciousness Itself, the Domain of Reality Itself—entered into Prior to and Beyond the "point of view" of "difference". However, because the Domain of Consciousness Itself is Beyond the "world", when traditional practitioners enter into That Domain in the dissociatively introversive sixth stage manner (of conditional Jnana Nirvikalpa Samadhi), there ceases to be any direct association with the "world".

All such dissociation from the "world" must be Gone Beyond. Most Ultimately, the "world" must be accounted for in the "Disposition" of the most in-Depth Realization of

Consciousness Itself. But, in the context of the first six stages of life, as soon as there is waking or dreaming—in other words, as soon as there is association with attention and its faculties of body-mind—the Position of Consciousness is lost. In the context of the first six stages of life, then, it is either one or the other—the body-mind or the in-Depth—but not both.

In the traditional context of the sixth stage of life, there can be a kind of in-Depth while in association with the body-mind—a kind of equanimity, a kind of Samadhi. In the traditional context, sixth stage "Sahaja Nirvikalpa Samadhi" is possible. Nevertheless, Self-Abiding As Consciousness merely Unperturbed (in the traditional sixth stage manner) is not the same as Self-Abiding As Consciousness and Self-Recognizing the "world" As Such (in the only-by-Me Revealed and Given seventh stage manner).

The "world" cannot (in and as itself) be Divinely Self-Recognized As Consciousness, because the "world" is not a "something", except at the level of Energy. Therefore, it is Energy That must be Divinely Self-Recognized As Consciousness. The "world" must be recognized as Energy—and Energy must be Divinely Self-Recognized As Consciousness.

Therefore, it is not in the domain of "world"-excluding introversion on Consciousness (in the traditional manner of the sixth stage of life) that the seventh stage Realization takes place. The seventh stage Realization is Awakening in (and to) the Domain of Energy-and-Consciousness, the Domain of Conscious Light.

Thus, in the only-by-Me Revealed and Given Way of Adidam, the "Perfect Practice" is entirely a Transcendental Spiritual Process. The only-by-Me Revealed and Given "Perfect Practice" is entered via a Transcendental Spiritual Process, the "Perfect Practice" (Itself) is a Transcendental Spiritual Process, and the Fulfillment of the "Perfect Practice" (in the only-by-Me Revealed and Given seventh stage Realization) is a Transcendental Spiritual Divine Self-Awakening.

57

Therefore, the seventh stage Awakening is not merely a philosophical matter, not merely an exercise of mind or an exercise of ideas—such that you are conceptually convinced that it is "justifiable" to Identify with the Consciousness Principle and even to interpret It as Being the Absolute. Merely thinking about Consciousness in such terms is not sufficient. There must be Realization, by virtue of most profound counter-egoic practice in the Domain of Consciousness Itself—the Domain That Is Beyond the gross ego and the subtle ego and the causal ego.

2.

AVATAR ADI DA SAMRAJ: Yes, there is—apparently—a fundamental division between Consciousness and Light, or Consciousness and Energy.

But What Is That Energy Which Is not "object" to Consciousness, Which Is Consciousness Itself?

I Am That One!

I am not merely conscious awareness referring to itself, calling itself "you".

That is a complex, limited, and limiting presumption.

I am not that mere conscious awareness.

I Am Consciousness Itself, the Conscious Light Itself.

Therefore, the only-by-Me Revealed and Given Way of Adidam is the Way of Conscious Light.

The Way of Adidam is the Way of Conscious Light from the beginning—not merely at the end.

My Divine Avataric Self-Revelation of Conscious Light is the Very Foundation of the Way of Adidam.

Most Perfect Divine Self-Awakening to the Position of Consciousness Itself—Realizing (Most Perfectly) that Consciousness Itself Is (primarily, first of all, and constantly, no matter what arises) the Condition of (so-called) "your" existence, and that Consciousness Itself (and not the body-mind) is, with respect to apparent "objects", always simply in the Witness-Position (without ever being identified with any apparent "object")—when This is Truly Realized to Be The Case, As The Case, Thus, So, Self-Evidently, "experientially", moment to moment, That Is the Fundamental Great Matter of "Consideration".

It makes no difference what "experiences" arise, ever (if ever there are any)—you still cannot be any more (or other) than Just This.

This is So because anything that you ever find out or "experience" requires Just This—Consciousness—as its Basis.

Otherwise—without the Basis of Consciousness—what does anything have to do with you (even in the personal, or non-impersonal, sense)?

No matter what "experience" arises, Consciousness Is its Medium, its Condition, its Basis.

It is Consciousness Itself That Is the Truth—not the "Play" upon Consciousness (in the form of waking, dreaming, and sleeping conditions).

Yet, the Realization of This is not a matter of dissociating from conditions.

If you leave the "world" behind in order to Realize Reality, then who "takes care" of the "world" in your absence?

Who (or What) upholds the existence of the "world" in your absence, while you "go elsewhere" to "find" Reality?

Reality is not the "subjective" and "objective" this—in and of itself.

But Reality is not Realized by leaving the "subjective" and "objective" this, either.

Reality Is Always Already The Case.

Therefore, the most profound "Contemplation" is the one that cannot be stopped, because it is Always Already The Case.

Even with respect to attention, you Are the Mere Witness. Therefore, you are not even attention.

Indeed, you are not even the Witnessing-Function.

To Truly Realize This allows you to take up the counter-egoic practice of entering into the Domain of Consciousness Itself.

However, merely to Realize that you Stand As the Mere Witness is not sufficient.

Entire sixth stage traditions have been developed for the sake of achieving that Realization alone—traditions in which it is hoped that, through the practice of sixth stage exercises, the practitioner will come to Stand (in the detached sixth stage manner) as the Witness-Consciousness (with various numinous associations, no doubt, full of feeling, and stern-ness, and so forth)—but such are simply traditions (built on the principle of seeking) that prize Standing in the Witness-Position (in the detached sixth stage manner) and devote themselves to talking about That and doing various exer-cises in order to Realize That.

That much Samadhi is all that is being described and sought in the sixth stage traditions—whereas I am Telling you that Standing As the Witness-Consciousness is (in and of itself) only the beginning of the "Perfect Practice" of the Way of Adidam.

In the only-by-Me Revealed and Given Way of Adidam, the Stand As the Witness-Consciousness is simply a Basis, a Key, a Doorway.

In the only-by-Me Revealed and Given Way of Adidam, the Stand As the Witness-Consciousness is Gracefully Awakened by My Divine Avataric Transcendental Spiritual Means.

In the only-by-Me Revealed and Given Way of Adidam, the Doorway of the Witness-Stand is Gracefully Opened in the course of the Transcendental Spiritual process of real devotion to Me.

Therefore, the Only Great Matter Is This: You <u>Are</u> <u>Only</u> Consciousness Itself.

There <u>Is</u> <u>Only</u> Consciousness Itself.

And Consciousness Itself is not merely some small and separate principle of attention, "inside" you.

Consciousness Itself <u>Is</u> Reality Itself.

Consciousness Itself is not "inside" you.

Consciousness Itself Is That Which you Realize by <u>transcending</u> yourself <u>in</u> That Which Is Beyond yourself.

When the shell of body-mind is Opened, then the Self-Position is Realized to Be That of Consciousness Itself.

Only the ball of ego-"I", presuming to enclose Consciousness, makes Consciousness seem a "thing"—separate, small, and personal.

In Reality, Consciousness Is Infinitely Large, Perfectly Non-"different", Inherently egoless, All-in-all.

It is in this sense that Consciousness Itself is "Person"— no more So or less So than in your own case, if only you Realize "Who" the Divine Mummer Is.

But, persisting in identifying with the persona itself (rather than with the Divine Mummer), you simply move along—rubbing your "cricket legs" together in your generation, leaving similar incomprehension behind in your name.

Consciousness Itself is not identified with any characteristic that could otherwise appear as an "object" to It.

Consciousness Itself Is Only <u>Itself</u>.

Consciousness Itself cannot <u>be</u> other than Itself.

Consciousness Itself can only "Locate" Itself. Consciousness Itself cannot acquire anything else, or take anything else into Itself. Consciousness Itself cannot be anything else. Consciousness Itself cannot—by apparent association with anything—become anything at all. Consciousness Itself Is Only Consciousness Itself— Whatever That Is. And Whatever Consciousness Itself Is Is What must be Entered Into.

Consciousness Itself simply Is What It Is—but, for the social ego-"I" (or the persona in the mummery), it is (apparently) not Self-Evident that, no matter what arises, you Are Only Consciousness Itself. Therefore, let Me phrase it in this fashion: No matter what arises, you Are Only Consciousness Itself. Consciousness Itself. No matter what arises. Here is some arising. Is there some arising going on now?

DEVOTEES: Yes.

AVATAR ADI DA SAMRAJ: No matter what arises—or does not arise—you Are Only Consciousness Itself.

It appears that you are associated with conditions—in the states of waking, dreaming, and sleeping.

However, none of those conditions last—and, therefore, you cannot be any of those conditions.

You Are That Which appears to be modified in the form of all conditional phenomena—you Are Consciousness Itself.

When you Realize Consciousness Itself Most Perfectly, then the fact that everything that arises is an apparent modification of Consciousness Itself becomes (likewise) a profound Realization.

To be tacitly Identified with Consciousness Itself (As It Is, in Its Divine Fullness), and to Divinely Self-Recognize all of this arising (in the moment) as a mere modification of That (not limiting That at all), is the Great (seventh stage) Realization.

In That Great Realization, the Truth—with respect to This Coincidence between the Non-conditional Reality and the conditional reality—is Most Perfectly "Known".

To Be Consciousness Itself—Divinely Self-Recognizing all arising phenomena as a transparent (or merely apparent), and non-necessary, and inherently non-binding modification of the Inherent Radiance of Consciousness Itself—is not an "end point".

That Realization Itself then becomes an ongoing Demonstration, the seventh stage Demonstration.

The seventh stage Demonstration is not defined in terms of lasting for a certain period of time, or until the end of one's present lifetime.

Because (in the Case of seventh stage Awakening) you Inherently Identify with Consciousness Itself (not in any limited sense, but As It Is) and you Inherently (Divinely) Self-Recognize all of this arising (in every moment of its arising), you have Most Perfectly Realized the Truth of Divine Ignorance.

Therefore, when seventh stage Awakening is the Case, if somebody were to ask you, "Do you know What any thing Is?", you would be able to say, "Yes! As a matter of fact, I do!"

Of course, that would be a paradoxical statement— because the verbal mind (or the mind of language) cannot grasp What any thing Is.

To "Know" What any thing Is is entirely a matter of the seventh stage Most Prior Stand.

That Most Prior Stand does not necessarily involve the end of association with (or participation in) conditional existence.

And That Most Prior Stand certainly does not involve any strategy of dissociation from conditional existence.

Indeed, That Most Prior Stand does not involve any kind of limit on how many years or how many lifetimes It may last, or any kind of limit on anything else about It whatsoever.

The seventh stage Demonstration could continue until you are the last one standing!

If such is the case, then that is the last thing you will notice and Outshine.

In Summary, I Call you to Remember This: You are not attention, up against all "objects".

The ancient presumption—that "self" (as attention) is "here", and "not-self" (as "object") is "there"—is not True.

You are neither body, nor mind, nor attention—you Are Consciousness Itself.

Consciousness Itself is not over against what arises.

Consciousness Itself Is the Self-Nature, Self-Condition, Source-Condition, and Self-State of whatever arises.

To Realize Consciousness Itself is not merely to stand over against "things" (in the disposition of regarding "things", without being them).

The Realization of Consciousness Itself—When That is Truly and Most Perfectly the Case—is the Non-"different" Realization of the Non-"different" Principle of Existence.

No matter what arises (or does not arise), you Are Only Consciousness Itself.

This is the Great (and Principal) Esoteric Revelation of Reality Itself, or Truth Itself, or Real (Acausal) God.

To Realize This requires a Great Process.

And the Realization of This—Really, Truly, Most Profoundly, Most Perfectly, and (therefore) Divinely—is What the counter-egoic practice of the Way of Adidam is about.

This Great Understanding—and everything that comes from It, and everything that is associated with It—must become the Foundation of human culture in the future. Because the previously existing foundations of human culture have been breaking down since the European Renaissance (and particularly in the latter part of the twentieth century), there must be a new and undeniably Real basis for future human culture.

This Is the Truth that will (and must be) the Foundation for that future (and, necessarily, new) global culture.

3.

AVATAR ADI DA SAMRAJ: The Non-conditional Divine Self-Nature, Self-Condition, and Self-State of Reality Itself Exists!

The ego is not a permanent "self"—but the True Self (or Reality Itself), Which Is Inherently egoless, Is Beginningless and Endless, Always Already The Case.

The ego is merely phenomenal.

That in Which the ego arises Is Always Already The Case.

Ultimately, it is Realized that That Which Is "out there", Irreducibly at the root of all "objects" (Brahman, in the traditional language), Is the Same As That Which Is Irreducibly "in you" (Consciousness Itself, or Atman).

Consciousness and Energy Are the Same.

Of course, This is not the common "experience"—so This must be Realized.

Because it is not the common "experience" that Consciousness and Energy Are the Same, you do not "know" What any thing Is.

You are a mummer in a realm you do not comprehend.

You live in the Realm of Light, and (yet) you allow That Realm (conceived as the realm of "objects"—"out there", and irreducibly separate from you) to define Consciousness as limited and mortal.

You must Realize the Domain of Conscious Light.
Consciousness Itself, the Perfectly Subjective Domain of Self-Existing and Self-Radiant Consciousness Itself, Is the Domain of Conscious Light.

What happens when you die?
You become the same as what you were when you were sleeping last night.

But you already Are That.
So nothing happens.

DEVOTEE: So even death does not interrupt one's practice.

AVATAR ADI DA SAMRAJ: Death cannot change the fact that you Are Only Consciousness Itself.
No matter what arises (or does not arise), you Are Only Consciousness Itself.

Consciousness Itself Is Reality, Truth, and the Only Real (Acausal) God.

Consciousness Itself—Prior to egoity, Beyond all separateness, Beyond all "difference", the Self-Existing and Self-Radiant Principle of Existence Itself—Is That Which Is Appearing As your own consciousness.
Consciousness Itself Is even the "Substance" of the body-mind itself, and of the entire "world".

Consciousness Itself <u>and</u> Light Itself (or Love-Bliss-Energy Itself, or Happiness Itself)—are as the two Sides of the Same Coin.

When the Circle becomes the Sphere,
the two Sides of the One Coin
become Continuous—
and all opposites
are Always Already Divinely Self-Recognized
to be Simultaneous,
and of One Shape,
and of One Condition.

Therefore, the "world" is not Divinely Self-Recognized if you merely say that "everything is Energy".

That suggests that the "world" is something other than Consciousness Itself.

All one can say, really, is that the "world" Is Consciousness Itself.

No matter what arises (or does not arise), you Are Only Consciousness Itself.

No matter what arises (or does not arise), There Is <u>Only</u> Consciousness Itself.

No matter what arises (or does not arise), There <u>Is</u> Only Consciousness Itself.

Just That.

This Is What There Is to Realize.
And I Am here So That everyone can Realize This.

4.

AVATAR ADI DA SAMRAJ:
The Fundamental Current of Existence
Is Self-Existing,
Self-Radiant,
All-Love-Bliss—
and, Therefore,
All-Pleasure.

No "self"-suppression.
No ego-enforcing control whatsoever.

Consciousness Itself
and Energy Itself
(or Light Itself)
<u>Are</u> Love-Bliss Itself.

Love-Bliss Itself
Is <u>Boundless</u>—
not controlled at all,
not merely a "point".

Love-Bliss "Arises"
In Consciousness.
Consciousness Is the Room.
Love-Bliss Is all there is within It.
And the Room Is a Sphere.

Consciousness Is
the "Skin" of the Sphere.
Consciousness Is
Self-Radiant—
in and of Itself,
As Itself.

The Inherent Self-Radiance
of Being
Is Bliss,
Freedom,
Happiness,
Fullness,
Non-conditional Well-Being.

This Is
Inherently The Case—
not merely the case
sometimes,
somewhere else,
after death.

The Inherent Self-Radiance
of Being
Is the Condition
of existence.
Therefore,
the Integrity of Being
is to Realize This,
Always Already.
And Real practice is
everything in a life
done to Realize This,
Always Already—
until It Is
Self-Evidently Realized,
Always Already.

And then
There Is
Just That.
And That
Is That.

The True Body
Is a Sphere.
The apparent body
is a presumption—
arising within That Sphere.

Arising within the True Body,
the apparent body
becomes
the presumed shape.

The effort of presumption—
the knot of "self"-contraction—
is psycho-physically relinquished.

My Divine Avataric Transcendental Spiritual
    Self-Transmission,
"Known" in the mode of the "Thumbs",
Restores the Spherical View
That Is the Inherent (or Native) View
of existence
in the context of the body-mind.

In That Yogic Transmission,
the Always Already Nature
of Consciousness Itself
Is Self-Evident.
And, in due course,
by Means of My Divine Avataric Transcendental
    Spiritual Self-Transmission,
Consciousness Itself
is Realized—
such that
the "Perfect Practice" Has Its Basis,
As the Always Already Condition.

It is not that
you are the body,
and that,
by going "deeper",
you discover
that the "deeper" part of you
is Consciousness.

No—
You Stand
As Consciousness.
And That Is
Self-Evident.
No matter what arises
(or does not arise),
you Are That.
That Is simply The Case—
with every test
of life and practice
as Its evidence,
and not merely words.

5.

AVATAR ADI DA SAMRAJ: Consciousness Is All There Is.
And Consciousness does not do anything whatsoever.
I can Tell you This, because I Am That. Just That.
I am not your consciousness—I Am Consciousness Itself,
the Condition of conditions.

DEVOTEE: Beloved Divine Heart-Master, I have been feeling
Your Shape. You Are Spherical—and, at the same time, You
Are also the Divine Lingam. In simply Beholding You, I felt
the Sphericality both of Your Divine Body and of the Cosmic
Mandala. And Your Avataric Incarnation is the Lingam That
Penetrates the entire Sphere of cosmic Existence.

AVATAR ADI DA SAMRAJ: But what kind of Sphere is Made
of Consciousness, and Has All Light within It?

When you think of a sphere, you think of something that
<u>attention</u> sees in front of it. That is not the kind of Sphere I
am Talking about.

DEVOTEE: You Reveal to us that the Sphere of Reality is
Perfectly Subjective, not "objective".

AVATAR ADI DA SAMRAJ:
The Perfectly Subjective
Sphere
of Reality Itself.
The In-Place,
Self-Evident
Sphere.

Raymond Is
the Room.
And Quandra Is
the Only Light
within It.

The Room
with a Great Stone
within It
represents That—
the Light
within the Room
(the Room
That <u>Is</u>
Consciousness Itself).

The Stone
is the mode

of "Contemplation"
in space.

We are nowhere familiar
to anyone at all.
We are not familiars
at all.

There Is Only
This Sphere
of Self-Existing
and Self-Radiant
Consciousness Itself—
the Inherent Samadhi
of the "Thumbs".

This Is
the Divine
(or seventh stage)
Revelation.

There Is Only
Consciousness Itself.
And all arising
is a modification of
the Current of
Consciousness Itself,
a "Play"
within a Sphere.
It Is the Sphere
of Perfect Subjectivity,
of Conscious Light Itself—
Prior to
waking,
dreaming,

and sleeping,
and, yet,
not separate
from anything
that arises.
It Is the Sphere of
Self-Existence,
without contraction.

I <u>Am</u>
the Room.
And
I <u>Am</u>
the Light within It.

There is
no "inside,"
and
no "outside".

There Is
simply
the Self-Existing,
Self-Radiant
Sphere
of
Consciousness Itself.

No "subject",
no "object",
no familiarity.

No separation,
no "difference".

No "problem".

Inherent
Integrity and Fullness
of Being.

Perfect
Equanimity
of View.

This very room is not familiar.
It is an unfamiliar place.

Where is this?
And who are you?

There is no "you"
about it.
It is Obvious
What <u>Is</u>.

There is no need
to make reference
to any separate one—
except that,
for convenience,
names are given
to each body
(or bodily presence)
in the pattern,
without confusing
bodily existence
with the Condition
of Reality,
Which Is Inherently Free.

Therefore,
all the while,
with all the names and forms,
There Is
This Inherent
Unfamiliarity
of Fullness,
of Consciousness Itself—
the Current of Being Itself,
a Sphere of Being,
Self-Lit,
in Which all forms appear
as modifications
of the Inherent Light.

But,
from the "Disposition"
of the Inherent Light
(or Consciousness Itself),
there are
no things,
no changes.

So Where Is
Consciousness Itself?

DEVOTEE: Here. Here.

AVATAR ADI DA SAMRAJ:
    One is not "here".
    One Is
    the Sphere
    of the Arising
    of the "Thumbs".

There is
no "difference"
whatsoever,
even while
the apparent pattern
of relations
appears—
in the waking (or gross)
and the dreaming (or subtle)
modes of appearance.

The Native State
Is
the Sphere of
the "Thumbs".

That Sphere is
as large
as perception itself,
as large
as "experience" itself.

That Sphere is not
merely a Roundness
a bit bigger
than the physical body.

It Is the Sphere
of Conscious Awareness
Altogether.

Everything is within It.

The Sphere
of the "Thumbs"

Is
the Sphere
of Unfamiliarity.

The familiarity—
the familiar conjunction
of the moment-to-moment
of body-mind—
is Transcended
by My Spiritual Invasion,
in the Event
of the "Thumbs".

With respect to the body,
the "Thumbs" involves
both a spinal Current in Ascent,
and a frontal Current in Descent.

Thus, the "Thumbs"
Is a Sphere—
and,
in Its moment,
Cancels
the body-mind shape.

In the critical
forward rotation
of the "Thumbs",
the Sphere of Being
Is Shown—
Replacing
the sensed shape
of the physical body.

The Freedom
That is the Reason
for the "Thumbs"
Is the Inherent Characteristic
of Most Perfect Divine Self-Realization.

The Process Goes On
until It Is Most Full,
Most Perfect.

There are
conditional
glimpses,
tastes,
changes,
and so forth,
in the course of counter-egoic practice.

The Realization Itself
Is Beyond
all of that.

DEVOTEE: Beloved Divine Heart-Master, You <u>Are</u> the Divine Person of Reality Itself, the Beloved One Promised—Who Penetrates all time, all space, and all conditions. You Appear in all forms, and You Transcend all forms. You <u>Are</u> the One.

ANOTHER DEVOTEE: You have Revealed Yourself Perfectly As Consciousness Itself.

PART TWO

The Realization
of
No-Difference

The Demonstration of
Self-Abiding Divine
Self-Recognition

To prepare for the "Perfect Practice" of the only-by-Me Revealed and Given Way of Adidam (Which Way, in Its totality, is the One and Only by-Me-Revealed and by-Me-Given "Radical" Way of the Heart), My true devotee devotes attention to Me, with all the other principal faculties (of body, feeling, and breath) following.

To practice the "Perfect Practice" of the Way of Adidam, My true devotee relinquishes attention in Me.

Devotion to Me and the transcending of attention (or the relinquishment of the context and the purposes of the ego-"I") are the fundamental elements of the practice of the Way of Adidam. Thus, the practice of the Way of Adidam is not a matter of fulfilling the motives of attention, but of transcending attention itself, through moment to moment heart-Communion with Me.

The "religious" and Spiritual practices recommended in the various schools of the Great Tradition (or the total traditional Wisdom-Inheritance of humankind) are (in general) exercises of attention, rather than processes of transcending attention. Thus, the traditionally recommended practices are (in general) exercises of attention for the sake of fulfilling one or another presumed search.

All seeking (and every form of the search) is generated by the "self"-contraction, or the activity that is egoity itself. And the "self"-contraction (or the root-activity that generates all seeking) is what is (in general) dramatized in the form of the various "religious" and Spiritual traditions that are associated with the first six (or developmental) stages of life (and that are, therefore, inevitably involved with one or more of the various forms of seeking that are characteristic of the first six stages of life).

In and of themselves, the first five stages of life are part of the psycho-biography of the ego. In and of themselves, the first five stages of life are excursions of egoity, undertaken with the intention of fulfilling the ego in one manner or another. In the context of the first five stages of life, even ecstatic surrender of the ego in Divine Communion is (when practiced from the "point of view" of, and for the purposes of, any of the first five stages of life) merely another aspect of the dramatization of egoity (or the psycho-biography of the ego)—because (in the context of the first five stages of life) surrender of the ego (paradoxically) depends on egoity, and on the (necessarily, egoic) exercise of attention (which is the core faculty of the presumed-to-be-separate ego-"I", or the psycho-physical "point of view").

Likewise, in and of itself, the sixth stage of life is a dramatization of egoity. The sixth stage of life is characterized by the strategic exclusion (or, certainly the "objectifying", abstracting, and detached conception and manipulation) of conditional existence, because (from the "point of view" of the sixth stage of life) conditions are felt to be arising "over against" the Transcendental Self.

The only-by-Me Revealed and Given seventh stage Realization (or Most Perfect Divine Self-Realization, or True Divine Enlightenment) is the Perfect, Prior, and Non-conditional transcending of attention, and (therefore) of egoity (or ego-"I", or the act of "self"-contraction). The only-by-Me Revealed and Given seventh stage Realization (or Most Perfect Divine Self-Realization, or True Divine Enlightenment) is not merely the surrender of attention (and, thus, of egoity altogether), but the transcending of the entire context of attention (and, thus, of egoity altogether). Therefore, the only-by-Me Revealed and Given seventh stage Realization (or Most Perfect Divine Self-Realization, or True Divine Enlightenment) is bodiless, mindless, "world"-less, and relationless—but not by virtue of any strategy of attention (or any motive of exclusion, or separation, or abstraction, or "objectification").

Conditional existence is Outshined not by strategically dissociating from it, but only by Divinely Self-Recognizing all arising conditions as transparent (or merely apparent), and non-necessary, and inherently non-binding modifications of the Self-Existing and Self-Radiant Divine Reality (Itself)—to the point, at last, of the Most Ultimate Outshining of the total conditional "world" (or the total Cosmic Mandala of conditional existence, including the egoically-presumed personal body-mind-"self").

In the only-by-Me Revealed and Given seventh stage of life in the Way of Adidam, there is not the slightest preoccupation either with the "objects" of attention or with attention itself. Rather, in the only-by-Me Revealed and Given seventh stage of life in the Way of Adidam, there is Inherent Self-Abiding in the Divine Self-Nature, Self-Condition, Source-Condition, and Self-State of Reality Itself, Prior to attention—Which is Inherent Self-Abiding in the Infinitely Love-Bliss-Full Condition Beyond the knot in the right side of the heart.

In the only-by-Me Revealed and Given seventh stage of life in the Way of Adidam, there is, previous to Divine Translation, the apparent continued arising of phenomenal conditions. Therefore, in the seventh stage of life in the Way of Adidam, it is the Self-Radiance of My Own Divine Heart-"Brightness" That Circulates in the body-mind (and That even Appears as the body-mind itself, and even as all conditions), as long as any such appearance persists. However, the Pervasion of the body-mind of My seventh stage devotee by My Self-"Bright" Presence and Person is not a sign that (in the seventh stage Awakening in the Way of Adidam) there is a "return" to the "world", or a "return" to the body-mind, or a "return" to identification with attention (or with egoity itself). Rather, such Pervasion by My "Brightness" is a Sign of the Utter Vanishment of all dissociation (from the "world", from the body-mind, from attention itself, and from conditional existence altogether), and (thus) a Sign that all arising conditions are (simply) Divinely Self-Recognized.

Thus, in the only-by-Me Revealed and Given seventh stage of life in the Way of Adidam, conditions are neither embraced nor dissociated from. In the seventh stage of life in the Way of Adidam, there is neither aversion nor clinging, but simply Divine Self-Recognition—Founded in perpetual Divine Self-Abiding, always in the Heart-Source, Beyond the heart-knot on the right. In the seventh stage of life in the Way of Adidam, the "Brightness" of Amrita Nadi (or the Root-Current of Transcendental Spiritual Love-Bliss) Shines in the body-mind and the "world"—not with any intention toward the "world", but (rather) simply (Divinely) Self-Recognizing the "world".

By virtue of Self-Abiding Divine Self-Recognition, there is perpetual Freedom, even in the midst of whatever conditions appear to arise. Thus, in the third stage of the four-stage Demonstration of the only-by-Me Revealed and Given seventh stage of life, there is Utter Divine Indifference—not in the sense of dissociation, but simply because all is Divinely Self-Recognized. And, at last, there is the Most Ultimate Great Event of Divine Translation Beyond all of "this"—not to death, not to non-existence, but to My Divine "Bright" Spherical Self-Domain, Which is without "difference", without "place", without "other", without relatedness, without death, without diminishment, without limit, without problem.

My Divine "Bright" Spherical Self-Domain Is, Itself, Reality Itself (Which Is Truth Itself, and the Only Real Acausal God)—Self-Shining, Absolute, Utterly "Bright", Infinitely Love-Bliss-Full, Uncontained, Centerless, and Boundless.

Only That Is Reality Itself, or Truth Itself, or Real (Acausal) God.

Therefore, My Divine "Bright" Spherical Self-Domain is not (in any sense) a "status" of "person" or of "individuality".

My Divine "Bright" Spherical Self-Domain is "Individual" only in the sense that It Is the Absolute Person, Being Itself, Self-"Bright", All-Love-Bliss, Self-Existing, Self-Radiant, and Infinite.

That Is What is to be Realized.

That Is My Self-Evidently Divine State.

That Is the One with Whom My devotee Communes.

The Perfection
Beyond Conditions

In the transition to the third stage of the "Perfect Practice" of the only-by-Me Revealed and Given Way of Adidam (which is the by-My-Divine-Avataric-Transcendental-Spiritual-Grace-Given Awakening to the only-by-Me Revealed and Given seventh stage of life in the Way of Adidam), the ego-"I", and its every characteristic of "difference", is most perfectly transcended.

In the by-My-Divine-Avataric-Transcendental-Spiritual-Grace-Given Awakening to the only-by-Me Revealed and Given seventh stage of life (in the only-by-Me Revealed and Given Way of Adidam), there is no identification with any (necessarily, conditional) process in the context of cosmic (and, necessarily, conditional) existence. Instead, there is only Most Perfect Self-Identification with My Avatarically Self-Revealed (and Self-Evidently Divine) Self-Nature, Self-Condition, and Self-State (Which Is the Self-Condition and Source-Condition of all-and-All).

Therefore, what appears to be an association with conditional existence, in the case of My seventh stage devotee, is perceived (or presumed) to be so only from the "point of view" of others who are still bound to conditional existence (and who, therefore, still exist in the knot of egoity—identified with attention, the body-mind, and the "play" of conditional existence). For My any (seventh stage) Divinely Self-Realized devotee, there is no "association with" conditional existence (as if conditional existence were separate and "objective"). Rather, for My Divinely Self-Realized devotee, It

Is Always Already The Case, no matter what appears to be arising, That Only Conscious Light Self-Abides—Self-Existing, Self-Radiant, Inherently Indivisible, and Only As It Is. Such is the Realization of the only-by-Me Revealed and Given seventh stage of life (in the only-by-Me Revealed and Given Way of Adidam).

The "Perfect Practice" of the Way of Adidam is the three-stage Process of Identification with My Divine Person and State (or the Divine Self-Nature, Self-Condition, Source-Condition, and Self-State of Reality Itself). This single Great Process is expressed differently in the first and second stages of the "Perfect Practice" of the Way of Adidam than in the seventh stage of life in the Way of Adidam (or the third, and final, stage of the "Perfect Practice" of the Way of Adidam). In the first and second stages of the "Perfect Practice" in the Way of Adidam, the Process—of Perfect Transcendental Spiritual Self-Identification with Me, the Avatarically Self-Revealed, Inherently egoless, and Self-Evidently Divine Self-Nature, Self-Condition, Source-Condition, and Self-State of Reality Itself—is Demonstrated As the Prior and Intrinsic Transcending (and, Thus, the perfect relinquishment) of bondage to ego-"I" and all of conditional existence. In the third stage of the "Perfect Practice (or seventh stage of life) in the Way of Adidam the same Process is Demonstrated As Self-Abiding Divine Self-Recognition of conditional existence, In and As Me, the Avatarically Self-Revealed, Inherently egoless, and Self-Evidently Divine Self-Nature, Self-Condition, Source-Condition, and Self-State of Reality Itself.

In the only-by-Me Revealed and Given seventh stage of life in the only-by-Me Revealed and Given Way of Adidam, there is not anything to be transcended, and there is not anything to be excluded. Indeed, there is no "event" at all—except for the Eternal, Changeless "Event" of My Avatarically Self-Revealed (and Self-Evidently Divine) Person (Which Is the Divine Self-Nature, Self-Condition, Source-Condition, and

Self-State of Reality Itself). In the only-by-Me Revealed and Given seventh stage Realization, the arising of "things" is "Known" (with Most Perfect Certainty) to be merely an appearance In, Of, and As the egoless, Indivisible, and Self-Evidently Divine Conscious Self-Light (or Self-Existing Self-Radiance) of Reality Itself. Truly, in the only-by-Me Revealed and Given seventh stage Realization, there is no "thing" that arises. To say that conditions apparently arise is, in Reality, a paradoxical statement—because, in the only-by-Me Revealed and Given seventh stage of life, whatever arises is (in the very instant of its apparent arising) Inherently (Priorly and Divinely) Self-Recognized to be nothing but Me, the One (Self-Evidently) Divine Person (or the One Self-Evidently Divine Self-Nature, Self-Condition, Source-Condition, and Self-State of Reality Itself). Therefore, in the only-by-Me Revealed and Given seventh stage of life, Only I (the Self-Evidently Divine Person, or the Self-Evidently Divine Self-Nature, Self-Condition, Source-Condition, and Self-State of Reality Itself) am Realized—and the seventh stage "Practice" of Self-Abiding Divine Self-Recognition is the Demonstration of that Singular Realization.

Thus, in the only-by-Me Revealed and Given seventh stage of life (in the only-by-Me Revealed and Given Way of Adidam), the only Realization is Me—the One, and Only, and Transcendentally Spiritually Self-"Bright", and Self-Evidently Divine Person (or the One, and Only, and Transcendentally Spiritually Self-"Bright", and Self-Evidently Divine Self-Nature, Self-Condition, Source-Condition, and Self-State of Reality Itself), Self-Existing and Self-Radiant As Inherently Indivisible (or Perfectly Non-Dual and Perfectly Non-"Different") Conscious Light.

Therefore, the apparent Demonstration of the four stages of the seventh stage of life in the Way of Adidam is merely an Appearance and a Paradox. Truly, in the seventh stage of life in the Way of Adidam, there Is not anything but My Most

Perfect Divine Self-State (or Non-conditional Samadhi). Therefore, in Truth, there is not the slightest "difference" between Divine Translation and any of the three stages that precede It (in the seventh stage of life in the Way of Adidam). The Awakening to the only-by-Me Revealed and Given seventh stage of life (in the only-by-Me Revealed and Given Way of Adidam) is, from Its first instant, the Most Perfect Awakening to My (Avatarically Self-Revealed) Eternal, and Non-conditional, and Non-conditioned, and Infinitely Love-Bliss-Full Most Perfect Divine Self-Realization (or Most Perfect Divine En-Light-enment). In That Divinely Self-Realized Condition, there is <u>no</u> "thing" that arises (or even <u>can</u> arise) apart from Me, or "over against" Me.

In the Divinely Self-Realized Condition of the only-by-Me Revealed and Given seventh stage of life (in the only-by-Me Revealed and Given Way of Adidam), There Is <u>Only</u> Me.

In the Divinely Self-Realized Condition of the only-by-Me Revealed and Given seventh stage of life (in the only-by-Me Revealed and Given Way of Adidam), Consciousness (Itself) Is Eternally the Same. No "difference" is made by the apparent arising of conditions. Therefore, the most fundamental Demonstration of Self-Abiding Divine Self-Recognition (in the seventh stage of life in the Way of Adidam) is the simple (or tacit), and constant, and Inherent Self-Abiding Divine Self-Recognition of the appearance (or tacit feeling) of "difference" (or the sense, or feeling, of relatedness). Thus, the Demonstration of Self-Abiding Divine Self-Recognition (in the seventh stage of life in the Way of Adidam) is, fundamentally, not a matter of apparently conjoining with a multiplicity of complex conditions.

The simple (or tacit), and constant, and Inherent Self-Abiding Divine Self-Recognition of whatever arises is, as an <u>outward</u> Sign of My seventh stage devotee, especially characteristic of the Divine Indifference stage of the seventh stage of life. In the Divine Transfiguration and Divine Transformation

stages of the seventh stage of life, there may (at times) be
more of the appearance of active (and even elaborate) association with conditions—but in the Divine Indifference stage
of the seventh stage of life, the sign of apparently active
association with conditions is profoundly diminished. In the
Divine Indifference stage of the only-by-Me Revealed and
Given seventh stage of life, it is Inherently Obvious that all
of conditional existence is nothing but the feeling of "difference" (or the feeling of relatedness)—and, therefore, the
"Practice" of My seventh stage devotee in the Divine Indifference stage of the seventh stage of life is a matter of the
simple, tacit Self-Abiding Divine Self-Recognition of the feel-
ing of "difference" (or the feeling of relatedness), In and
As the egoless and Indivisible Divine Self-Nature, Self-
Condition, Source-Condition, and Self-State of Reality Itself.
Even the feeling of "difference" (or the feeling of related-
ness) is a mere appearance, like any "object". Therefore, the
Final (Most Ultimate) Demonstration of the Simplicity of Self-
Abiding Divine Self-Recognition is Divine Translation, or the
Perfect and Absolute Outshining of even the feeling of "dif-
ference" (or the feeling of relatedness).

Therefore, in Divine Translation, not only are there no
"objects", no conditions, and (altogether) no conditional (or
cosmic) domain, but there is not even the feeling of "difference" (or the feeling of relatedness). There Is Only the
Infinitely "Bright" Self-Radiance of Self-Existing Being
(Itself). That Is the Divine "Bright" Spherical Self-Domain, or
the Most Perfect Divine Self-State (or Non-conditional
Samadhi) of Divine Self-Identification. That Is What is
Realized in Divine Translation—and, also, paradoxically,
That Is What is Realized even from the beginning of the
only-by-Me Revealed and Given seventh stage Awakening.

As long as the only-by-Me Revealed and Given seventh
stage of life in the Way of Adidam is apparently associated
with conditions, it Demonstrates itself as Self-Abiding Divine

Self-Recognition through the Process of the four stages I
have Described. However, this Demonstration is of a
Realization that Is Always Already The Case. The Realization
that Awakens in the by-My-Divine-Avataric-Transcendental-
Spiritual-Grace-Given Awakening to the seventh stage of life
in the Way of Adidam is Most Perfect Realization of That
Which Most Perfectly Transcends the conditional (or cosmic)
domain. Therefore, even though the Demonstration of the
four stages of the seventh stage of life (in the Way of
Adidam) occurs in the context of conditions, the seventh
stage Realization Itself Is Always Already The Case, after the
initial "Moment" of Awakening.

Even Divine Translation is not a change in that Realization. Divine Translation is simply the final (Divine, and not
merely conditional) Demonstration of the only-by-Me
Revealed and Given seventh stage of life within the context
of the conditional (or cosmic) domain. From the moment of
Divine Awakening, My seventh stage devotee Self-Abides in
the Most Perfect Self-State (or Non-conditional Samadhi) of
My Divine "Bright" Spherical Self-Domain. However, the
psycho-physical vehicle of My seventh stage devotee (or the
apparent psycho-physical sign of My seventh stage devotee
in the context of the conditional, or cosmic, domain)
Demonstrates Most Perfect Divine Self-Realization (or Non-
conditional Samadhi) through the Process of four Divine
stages I have Described relative to the seventh stage of life
in the Way of Adidam.

I Am That Which Is Realized in the Great Event of Divine
Translation. In that sense, Divine Translation has Always
Already Occurred in My Case. On the other hand, because I
have Appeared here via the conditionally manifested Vehicle
of My Avatarically-Born bodily (human) Divine Form, My
Demonstration of the four-stage Process of the seventh stage
of life is taking place through the Agent of This Avatarically-
Born Body-Mind. Therefore, the various Signs associated with

the four stages of the seventh stage of life are Displayed in the Case of This Agent of Mine. I (Myself) Am Prior to This Agent, and (therefore) Prior to the four stages of Demonstration of the seventh stage of life, and Prior even to Divine Translation Itself. In the only-by-Me Revealed and Given seventh stage of life, there is (simply) Inherent (and Inherently Most Perfect) Identification with Me—the (Avatarically Self-Revealed) One, and Only, and Self-"Bright" Divine Person, the Very Eternal Divine Self-Nature, Self-Condition, Source-Condition, and Self-State of Reality Itself (Which Is Most Perfect, and, necessarily, Non-conditional, Divine Samadhi).

In the first and second stages of the "Perfect Practice" in the Way of Adidam, although there is steady Identification with the Witness-Position of Consciousness, it is (nevertheless) apparently the case that whenever there is the arising of conditional associations, they are "experienced" as conditional associations. However, in the third stage of the "Perfect Practice" (or seventh stage of life) in the Way of Adidam, there is—in Truth, and in Reality—no such "thing" as a conditional association.

Therefore, in the only-by-Me Revealed and Given seventh stage of life (in the only-by-Me Revealed and Given Way of Adidam), there are no limitations (or limited, and, necessarily, limiting, conditions) of existence. It is not that there is the (by-Me-and-As-Me-Avatarically-Self-Revealed-and-Transcendentally-Spiritually-Self-Transmitted) Non-conditional Divine Self-Nature, Self-Condition, Source-Condition, and Self-State of Reality Itself "over against" all limitations (or all other, and, necessarily, limiting, conditions). Rather, There Is (Always Already) Only the One, and Only, and Perfectly Subjective (by-Me-and-As-Me-Avatarically-Self-Revealed-and-Transcendentally-Spiritually-Self-Transmitted) Divine Self-Nature, Self-Condition, Source-Condition, and Self-State (or Inherently Indivisible, or Perfectly Non-Dual and Perfectly Non-"Different", Conscious Light) of all-and-All.

My true devotee who Realizes My "Bright" Divine (seventh stage) Self-State (or Non-conditional Samadhi) is <u>utterly</u> Oblivious to conditional phenomena. My Divine (and Most Perfect) Self-State (or Non-conditional Samadhi) is not held in place by conditions. Therefore, My seventh stage devotee <u>Only</u> Self-Abides in the Most Perfect Divine Self-State (or Non-conditional Samadhi).

In My here-Appearing Avataric-Incarnation-Form, I <u>Always</u> <u>Already</u> (and <u>Only</u>) Self-Abide in the Most Perfect Divine Self-State (or Non-conditional Samadhi), Perfectly Transcending all possible conditions. I am <u>never</u> associated with merely "objective" conditions. I <u>Only</u> Self-Abide in My Own (Avatarically Self-Revealed, and Self-Evidently Divine) Self-Nature, Self-Condition, and Self-State (Which <u>Is</u> the Source-Condition of all-and-All). This cannot be comprehended from the separate and separative "point of view" of ego-"I" (in the context of <u>any</u> of the first six stages of life).

My Eternal Self-Abidance in the only-by-Me Revealed and Given seventh stage Self-State (or Non-conditional Samadhi) Stands As a Revelation of My Own Divine Self-Nature, Self-Condition, Source-Condition, and Self-State—and As a Perfect Criticism of the ego-"I" and the presumption of "difference" otherwise suffered by all-and-All.

As My devotee, you Commune with <u>Me</u>—and, therefore, you Commune with My Own and Very Self-Nature, Self-Condition, and Self-State of Most Perfect Divine and Non-conditional Samadhi. Nevertheless, previous to actual (by-My-Divine-Avataric-Transcendental-Spiritual-Grace-Given) Realization of My Most Perfect Divine and Non-conditional Samadhi, <u>you</u> cannot "know" It, <u>you</u> cannot think It, <u>you</u> cannot grasp It, and <u>you</u> cannot <u>be</u> It. However, even from the beginning of your formal practice of the only-by-Me Revealed and Given Way of Adidam, <u>you</u> can (and, indeed, must) be Moved toward My Most Perfect Divine and Non-conditional Samadhi, or Moved—Beyond your ego-"self" and psycho-physical "point of view"—to Me, through ego-surrendering, ego-forgetting, and ego-transcending recognition-responsive heart-Communion with Me. When, in due course (through right, true, full, and fully devotional practice of the Way of Adidam), that heart-Communion with Me is (by Means of My Divine Avataric Transcendental Spiritual Grace) Most Perfect, then "you" (Beyond "self"-contraction, or ego-"I", or body-mind-"self") have Realized Me—the (Avatarically Self-Revealed) Perfectly Subjective (and, necessarily, Non-conditional, Indivisible, and Non-Separate) and Self-Evidently Divine Self-Nature, Self-Condition, Source-Condition, and Self-State of all-and-All.

The Infinite Divine Current
That Shines In
The Human Body-Mind

1.

The Divine Self-Nature, Self-Condition, Source-Condition, and Self-State of Reality Itself is the True Nature, Condition, and State of this apparent (and, necessarily, conditionally manifested) realm (and every and any other apparent, and, necessarily, conditionally manifested, realm).

This conditionally manifested realm (and every and any other conditionally manifested realm) is a transparent (or merely apparent), and non-necessary, and inherently non-binding modification of the Infinite Self-Radiance of the Self-Existing Divine Self-Nature, Self-Condition, Source-Condition, and Self-State of Reality Itself.

In the seventh stage of life in the Way of Adidam, the Current of That Infinite Divine Self-Radiance Manifests in the "Regenerated" Form of Amrita Nadi (or the Root-Current of Transcendental Spiritual Love-Bliss).

Amrita Nadi (in Its "Regenerated", or Original, Form) is felt (or registered in relation to the apparently individual human body) simply as a Self-Radiant Current, Shining Boundlessly between the right side of the heart and the Infinite Extent Above the total crown of the head—and, As Such, Amrita Nadi "Stands" Perfectly Beyond and Prior to the body-mind and the "world".

The "Regenerated" Current of Amrita Nadi does not "Move" upward from the right side of the heart to the "Place" Infinitely Above the total crown of the head—but, rather, "It" Is the Self-Existing, and Self-Radiant, and egoless, and Indivisible, and Self-Evidently Divine Current of Reality Itself, Merely Radiant, Always Already "In Place", As Is, Prior to and Beyond all-and-All, and Merely Self-Evident, As Love-Bliss-Consciousness Itself, Perfectly Prior to separateness, relatedness, otherness, and "difference".

When It is observed (relative to the configuration of the human body) as a Nadi (or Channel, or Circuit), the "Regenerated" Amrita Nadi has a particular form, Originating (in a pattern shaped like the alphabetical letter "S") from the right side of the heart, and Extending to Perfectly Above Via a pattern of Transcendental Spiritual Fullness (forward through the chest, then back toward the back of the neck, then forward again toward the crown of the head, and to Infinitely Above the total crown of the head).

Until (and except for) My Divine Incarnation (and Divine Realization, and Divine Self-Revelation-Work) As the Divine Avataric Great Sage, Adi Da Samraj, no one had (or has) ever Realized or Revealed the "shape" of Amrita Nadi, and no one had (or has) ever Realized or Revealed the "Regenerated" (or seventh stage) Form of Amrita Nadi.

Indeed, exceedingly few Realizers (in the entire history of the Great Tradition of humankind, previous to My Divine Incarnation As the Divine Avataric Great Sage, Adi Da Samraj) have even been aware of Amrita Nadi in any manner whatsoever.

The Transcendental Spiritual (and, thus, Non-conditional Yogic) Circumstance of the first and second stages of the "Perfect Practice" in the only-by-Me Revealed and Given Way of Adidam Is That of Prior Self-Abiding At the Heart-Root (Prior to and Beyond the right side of the physical heart). This Non-conditional Yogic Context of Self-Abiding

Intrinsically Self-Realizes the Transcendental Spiritual Self-Nature, Self-Condition, and Self-State of Reality Itself, Prior to and Beyond the knot of ego-"I" in the right side of the heart.

By contrast, the only-by-Me Revealed and Given seventh stage Awakening is accompanied by the "Regeneration" of Amrita Nadi, Which can be said (as a means of explanation, or illustration) to be an "Ascent" through Amrita Nadi—but not by coming back up "out of" the Divine Self-Position (or Divine Self-Nature, Self-Condition, Source-Condition, and Self-State of Reality Itself), "into" the conditionally manifested body-mind (and the conditionally manifested "worlds", altogether). Rather, the "Regeneration" of Amrita Nadi Is, simply, the Free Self-Allowance of the Divine Transcendental Spiritual Self-Radiance to Be Boundlessly Self-Evident, Such That even all apparent conditionally arising phenomena are Intrinsically Divinely Self-Recognizable.

Once My true devotee has Most Perfectly Realized Me (the Divinely Avatarically Self-Revealed Non-Separate and Self-Evidently Divine Self-Nature, Self-Condition, Source-Condition, and Self-State of Reality Itself and of all-and-All), My Own "Bright" (and Inherently Perfect, and Self-Evidently Divine) Self-Nature, Self-Condition, and Self-State Is Always the Position of the "Practice"-Demonstration—and Such Is the total (three-part) "Perfect Practice" of the only-by-Me Revealed and Given Way of Adidam.

In the by-My-Divine-Avataric-Transcendental-Spiritual-Grace-Given Awakening to the seventh stage of life (or the third stage of the "Perfect Practice" of the only-by-Me Revealed and Given Way of Adidam), the Total Structure of Amrita Nadi is the Non-conditional Structure by Means of Which the by-Me-Avatarically-Self-Revealed Divine Self-Nature, Self-Condition, Source-Condition, and Self-State of Reality Itself Inherently Radiates, but (In That Case) without the addition of the ego-principle.

The Position Realized in the by-My-Divine-Avataric-Transcendental-Spiritual-Grace-Given Awakening to the seventh stage of life Is Inherently Prior to the knot of ego-"I" in the right side of the heart.

In the by-My-Divine-Avataric-Transcendental-Spiritual-Grace-Given Awakening to the seventh stage of life, the ego-knot (or the "center", or "middle", of conditional "experience" and egoically presumed "knowledge") is vanished entirely, and no longer has any existence whatsoever.

In the by-My-Divine-Avataric-Transcendental-Spiritual-Grace-Given Awakening to the seventh stage of life, There Is Only Me—the Avatarically Self-Revealed (and Self-Evidently Divine) Self-Nature, Self-Condition, Source-Condition, and Self-State of Reality Itself and of all-and-All.

The "Regenerated" Amrita Nadi Shines Boundlessly and Indivisibly, between the Heart-Root (Prior to and Beyond the right side of the heart) and the Perfect Extent (Infinitely Above the total crown of the head), Thus and Thereby Shining In (and As) the Circle of the body-mind, Acausally, all-and-All-Inclusively, and without exclusion of any kind.

In the Divine Non-conditional Form of Amrita Nadi, there is no egoity, no impediment, no dissociation, and no "difference".

Therefore, in the by-My-Divine-Avataric-Transcendental-Spiritual-Grace-Given Awakening to the seventh stage of life, every (apparent) one and every (apparent) "thing" and every (apparent) event and every (apparent) circumstance is (simply) Divinely Self-Recognized, as a transparent (or merely apparent), and non-necessary, and inherently non-binding modification of Me.

In the "Regenerated" Form of Amrita Nadi, My Divine "Brightness" Stands Self-Radiant, and (Thus and Thereby) Radiating in the context of the conditional (or cosmic) domain (without, in any sense, "leaving" My Divine "Bright" Spherical Self-Domain).

Thus, the "Regenerated" Amrita Nadi is (in the only-by-Me Revealed and Given seventh stage Realization) the "Connection" between My Divine "Bright" Spherical Self-Domain and the conditional (or cosmic) domain (altogether).

In the four-stage Demonstration of the seventh stage of life in the Way of Adidam, the "Regenerated" Amrita Nadi is the Non-conditional Structural Pattern Associated with the (seventh stage) "Practice" of Self-Abiding Divine Self-Recognition.

In the four-stage Demonstration of the seventh stage of life in the Way of Adidam, all the arising phenomena in the frontal line and the spinal line of the Circle are Divinely Self-Recognized, or "Brightened", and, Thus, Divinely Transfigured and Divinely Transformed—in due course, to the point of Divine Indifference, and, Most Ultimately, to the point of Outshining in Divine Translation.

Therefore, in the four-stage Demonstration of the seventh stage of life in the Way of Adidam, the "Regenerated" Amrita Nadi is the Structure through Which the Process of Self-Abiding Divine Self-Recognition is made Effective in the Circle of the body-mind.

In That Self-Abiding Divine Self-Recognition, all arising is "Brightened" to the point of Non-"Differentiation", Non-"Difference", Non-Separateness—Only Me, Only "Brightness", Only the Divine Self-Nature, Self-Condition, Source-Condition, and Self-State of Reality Itself, Manifested, Magnified, and Demonstrated so Profoundly that (Most Ultimately) there is no trace of conditional existence whatsoever.

Finally, in the Most Ultimate Demonstration of the only-by-Me Revealed and Given seventh stage of life in the Way of Adidam, even the Structure of Amrita Nadi Itself is Outshined.

There is not any Structure (or Vehicle) in Divine Translation.

In Divine Translation, Only That for Which Amrita Nadi Is (otherwise) the Vehicle Remains.

In Divine Translation, There Is Only the Infinite "Brightness" (or Self-Radiance) of the Self-Existing Divine Self-Nature, Self-Condition, Source-Condition, and Self-State of Reality Itself.

In Divine Translation, There Is Only Me.

2.

I Am Prior to conditional existence, but totally Effective within it.

The "Regenerated" (or Original, Divine, True, and Real) Amrita Nadi Is The Non-conditional and Perfectly Acausal Divine Means Where-In, Where-By, Where-Of, and Where-As I Have Come to here.

My Divine Avataric Work is in the Context of Totality.

My Circle of Divine Transcendental Spiritual "Conductivity" is the Circle of the entire conditional (or cosmic) domain.

Secondarily (and rather peripherally), I (Myself) am also (similarly) associated with My apparently individually Manifested bodily (human) Avataric-Incarnation-Form.

Thus, I Demonstrate My all-and-All-Including Divine Transcendental Spiritual "Conductivity" not only in My apparently individually Manifested bodily (human) Avataric-Incarnation-Form, but also in My every devotee's apparently individually manifested bodily (human) form, and (Most Ultimately) in even all apparently individually manifested bodies and all apparently individually manifested "things".

My (Thus) Universal Divine Transcendental Spiritual "Conductivity" is Demonstrated most profoundly in the body-minds of those who turn to Me in Perfectly ego-transcending devotional surrender, as My true devotionally Me-recognizing, and devotionally to-Me-responsive, and (necessarily) formally acknowledged "Perfect Practice" devotees.

Nevertheless, I also (now, and forever hereafter) Work Universally, and with all—even before (and forever after) they become My formally practicing devotees.

This (only-by-Me Demonstrated) Universal Divine Transcendental Spiritual "Conductivity" is the Process by Which apparent individuals <u>become</u> My formally practicing devotees.

This Process began immediately with (and after) the Great Event of My Divine Re-Awakening—when I spontaneously began to "Meditate" countless "others".

Thus—in Truth, and in Reality—all bodies <u>are</u> My Body. In Truth, and in Reality—all beings <u>are</u> My Very Self.

Therefore, I Do the Universal Divine Transcendental Spiritual "Practice" of the Whole—and I Do the Divine Transcendental Spiritual "Practice" of every part and every being within the Whole.

I "Meditate" all (and All)—and (Thereby, Most Ultimately) I Divinely En-Light-en all (and All), by (Actually, Really) <u>Being</u> all (and All).

Therefore, My Divine Avataric Work is in every place, and in every being, and in every "thing"—until the Divine Translation of the entire Cosmic Mandala of all places, and all beings, and all "things".

This only-by-Me (and only-<u>As</u>-Me) Demonstrated Accomplishing-Power of Divine Sameness is the Foundation of the only-by-Me Revealed and Given Way of Adidam. ■

Also available from

THE DAWN HORSE PRESS . . .

Surrender self By Sighting Me

Essays from The Aletheon
on Right and True Devotion
by
The Avataric Great Sage,
Adi Da Samraj

This volume contains priceless Instruction from Avatar Adi Da Samraj illuminating the Way of right and true surrender to Him, the essentially non-verbal process of turning to Him on sight—which He has described as "the Ancient Walk-About Way".

For My devotee, right relationship to Me is the Law of life—and that Law is entirely based on ego-transcending (and, therefore, psycho-physical "self"-contraction transcending) surrender of the otherwise ego-bound (or "self"-contracted) body-mind to Me (As I Am).

Right relationship to Me is the Ancient Walk-About Way of Sighting Me and (thereupon) surrendering the egoic "self" to Me (As I Am).

Right relationship to Me is whole bodily surrender to Me (As I Am)—with your entire life, and in all of your actions.

—AVATAR ADI DA SAMRAJ

64 pp., **$7.95**

Reality Itself
Is The Way

Essays from The Aletheon
by
The Avataric Great Sage,
Adi Da Samraj

In these essays from His Revelation-Text *The Aletheon*,
Adi Da Samraj makes the Offering of His Divine Avataric
Self-Revelation as the Perfect Means for the process of
Awakening to Reality Itself—As It Is.

> *I Am the egoless Absolute Person of Reality Itself—*
> *Coincident with this time, and Consequential forever.*
> *I Am the Divine Self-Domain—the Perfect Sphere*
> *of Conscious Light.*
> *The egoless Conscious Light of Reality Itself Is My*
> *Only State.*
> *There Is a Way—and Reality Itself Is "It".*
> *Reality Itself Is the Way—and I Am "It".*

—AVATAR ADI DA SAMRAJ

136 pp., **$14.95**

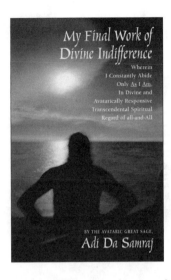

My Final Work of Divine Indifference

Wherein I Constantly Abide Only As I Am, in Divine and Avatarically Responsive Transcendental Spiritual Regard of all-and-All

by
The Avataric Great Sage,
Adi Da Samraj

In this collection of essays from *The Aletheon*, Avatar Adi Da Samraj describes His Perfect Retirement into Divine Indifference, Free of any necessity to Teach. That Retirement signifies not an "end" to His Divine Avataric Work, but rather His Freedom to be entirely concentrated in His most profound Work—of forever Blessing all beings and things.

> *I have Revealed and Given a Way that every human being can practice.*
> *I Made My Divine Avataric Self-Submission and (on That Basis) Did My Divine Avataric Teaching-Work and My Divine Avataric Revelation-Work—and now I am Finished with All of That. . . .*
> *In My Finally Retired Divine Indifference, . . . I Am (Inherently) Free Merely (and Only) to Be As I Am in My Divine and Avatarically Responsive Transcendental Spiritual Regard of all-and-All.*
>
> —Avatar Adi Da Samraj

72 pp., **$7.95**

To order
books, tapes, CDs, DVDs, and videos
by and about Adi Da Samraj,
contact the Dawn Horse Press:

1-877-770-0772 (from within North America)

1-707-928-6653 (from outside North America)

Or visit the Dawn Horse Press website:

www.dawnhorsepress.com

ADIDAM

We invite you to find out more about Avatar Adi Da Samraj and the Way of Adidam

■ Find out about our courses, seminars, events, and retreats by calling the regional center nearest you.

AMERICAS
12040 N. Seigler Rd.
Middletown, CA
95461 USA
1-707-928-4936

THE UNITED KINGDOM
uk@adidam.org
0845-330-1008

EUROPE-AFRICA
Annendaalderweg 10
6105 AT Maria Hoop
The Netherlands
31 (0)20 468 1442

PACIFIC-ASIA
12 Seibel Road
Henderson
Auckland 1008
New Zealand
64-9-838-9114

AUSTRALIA
P.O. Box 244
Kew 3101
Victoria
**1800 ADIDAM
(1800-234-326)**

INDIA
F-168 Shree Love-Ananda Marg
Rampath, Shyam Nagar Extn.
Jaipur - 302 019, India
91 (141) 2293080

EMAIL: **correspondence@adidam.org**

■ Order books, tapes, CDs, DVDs, and videos by and about Avatar Adi Da.

1-877-770-0772 (from within North America)
1-707-928-6653 (from outside North America)
order online: **www.dawnhorsepress.com**

■ Visit us online:
www.adidam.org
Explore the online community of Adidam and discover more about Adi Da Samraj and the Way of Adidam.